RUGBY DRILLS

125 ACTIVITIES TO IMPROVE YOUR COACHING SESSIONS

Eamonn Hogan

THE CROWOOD PRESS

First published in 2014 by
The Crowood Press Ltd
Ramsbury, Marlborough
Wiltshire SN8 2HR

www.crowood.com

This impression 2018

British Library Cataloguing-in-Publication Data
A catalogue record for this book is available from the British Library.

ISBN 978 1 84797 655 0

Acknowledgements
This book would not have been made possible without the kindness and hard work of many throughout the last twenty-plus years who really deserve to have their contributions noted here but for brevity reasons, I will name check just a few.

In the USA, I would like to thank Paul Holmes, Tom Rooney, the citizens of Obetz and Columbus Ohio, Luke Gross, Kevin Battle, Ben Parker, Paul Keeler, Lisa Rosen, Danielle Miller, Kathy Flores, Brett Mills, Coilin Jones, Sean O'Leary, Dr Steve Durant, Bruce Maclane, Mike Tolkin, Bob Weir, Lance Connolly, Mike Diamantopoulous, Dan Payne, Scott Lawrence, John Connolly, Drew Fautley, Michael Engelbrecht and Will 'Salty' Thompson. And the inimitable Paule and Ann Barford – among the top five coolest people I have ever met.

Thanks to Andy and Debbie Byrne, the best rugby administrators I know and to the players, coaches, referees and administrators of Lincoln RFC for the kindness they have shown my family over the years

At Leicester Tigers, from both the past and the present I would like to thank the following: Dusty Hare, Andy Key, Neil McCarthy, Carl Douglas, Graham Rowntree, Neil Back, Mike Penistone, Richard Cockerill, Pat Howard and Scott Clarke. Final thanks must go to the one person who spent most of her time over my five years at Tigers stopping me from making a complete fool of myself – Teresa Carrington, thank you so much.

Thanks to Dan Cottrell at Green Start Media whose confidence in me led to my meeting with the Crowood Press.

To my brother Sean and his wife Trish and to my parents Mary and Thomas Hogan – my passion for sport, my love of family and the belief that I could achieve far more than my education may suggest, are all down to you. To my sons Brandon and Ewan – you continually make us laugh and fill us with pride with everything that you do.

Finally, to my wife Samantha. – mother, MSc, rugby coach, rugby referee, hockey umpire, paramedic, university lecturer, advisor to the RFU and published author. All of this and she still has time to stop me killing our children with poorly cooked food. Thank you for being the most significant part of my life.

Typeset by Jean Cussons Typesetting, Diss, Norfolk

Printed and bound in India by Replika Press Pvt Ltd

Contents

Introduction

In my time as a rugby coach, the one phrase that has annoyed me the most is, 'Rugby is a simple game, really.' If it is a simple game, why are there five levels of rugby coaching award in the UK?

Rugby is really not a simple game, no more than chess is simply a matter of moving a few strange-looking figures around a board. Getting across to a new player the simple idea of running forward and passing backwards can attest that 'simple' isn't really a word that springs to mind. With patience, understanding and a willing participant, play does improve with practice. Over time, a greater appreciation of those who do play rugby with a reasonable degree of skill soon becomes apparent.

As difficult as it is to play rugby, many assume the major challenges are over once they decide to step into the spotlight and become a coach. Coaching any sport is a significant challenge that can be aided by having played that sport but, for many coaches, their children or their partners drew them to rugby so they may not have any real background in rugby to call upon. It is in these cases, where the parent or player has stepped into a new role in rugby, that this book becomes invaluable.

When people attend coaching courses, they do so with the understanding that they need to progress their own skills and knowledge to aid the growth of their own team. What isn't so forthcoming on these courses is how to maintain a level of energy about your sessions over the course of several seasons following that original qualification.

There are many challenges put before a coach but primary among them is the desire to keep reinforcing the same positive ideas in new and imaginative ways, which is where this book can help you the most.

This book has been written in an easy-to-read format along with well-developed and thought-out activities that will aid you in getting your messages across to your team while also making them think carefully about what it takes to complete the challenges you have placed in front of them. Many were created by myself but some have been used by the most famous coaches in the world and I have made them much more user-friendly for the development of players in rugby.

These activities were designed for you to use without the need of purchasing specialist and expensive equipment, as all that is required to complete the activities within this book are a few basics available to every rugby coach within a club or school:

■ Willing players
■ A number of rugby balls
■ Cones of various colours
■ A few tackle shields
■ A few tackle bags
■ A stopwatch
■ A whistle

This book is designed to sit next to your laptop or in your home, to find that drill that really nails what you want to achieve from the next session with your team.

The book does not pontificate on why a drill needs to be used, why your team should use it, or when it needs to be put into place in your season; it simply passes on the drill, with a very straightforward explanation of what is required without trying to make them out to be more than they are.

Remember, you are the coach of your team and although there are many books that can tell you how to coach, this book assumes you know your team better than anyone else and what you really need is a resource to emphasize a point to them in an imaginative way – that's it.

I hope you and your team enjoy the drills in this book and I wish you continued success.

KEY TO SYMBOLS USED IN THIS BOOK

ATTACKER (VARIOUS COLOURS)

POSITION OF PLAYER BEFORE MOVING

DEFENDER

MARKER CONE

TACKLE TUBE

TACKLE SHIELD

PASS/KICK

PLAYER RUNNING WITH BALL

DIRECTION OF MOVEMENT WITHOUT BALL

BOUNCE/MOVEMENT OF BALL

RUGBY BALL

CONTACT

COACH

MARKER CONES OF VARIOUS COLOURS

RUNNING DIRECTION AROUND A CONE/TUBE

SKI POLES

SCRUM/SCRUM MACHINE

CHAPTER 1 – THE WARM-UP

This chapter contains the following drills designed to facilitate warm-up sessions.

Sprint Relays

Leg and Lower Back Warm-Up for Rucking

Physical Intensity

Pre-Match Warm-Ups

Ruck Warm-Up on Hard Ground

Use the Field (1): Aerobic Runs

Use the Field (2): Aerobic Interval Training

Use the Field (3): Chase Sprints

Use the Field (4): Staggered Sprints

Use the Field (5): Dynamic Warm-Up Channels

CHAPTER 1

The Warm-up

In 1991, I went on my first coaching course courtesy of the Royal Air Force and I was the youngest by twelve years. On arrival, we assembled on the side of the field, put our boots on and waited for the lead tutor to appear and dazzle us.

He duly arrived with a big smile on his face and asked me to think of a number between one and thirty… I said ten. 'Ten laps of the field it is, boys – off you go!' Off we went and as a fairly fit rugby player at that time, I was back and sitting down in no time, but for my retired, ex-prop colleagues the same could not be said. It took forty-five minutes for them to return and the tutor just stood there reading his notes, occasionally talking to ones that had finished about the recent matches they had seen or did they know so-and-so from such a team. No mercy shown.

When the final man arrived back, he asked me to pick a number between one and twenty. Learning from the last time I immediately said 'One'. 'Right, that's one minute's rest and we are straight into the basics of handling!' The next hour and twenty minutes were hell on earth for the older guys on the course. They kept dropping the ball, running for water and missing their turn in drills. It was an absolute shambles. Finally, he blew the whistle and dismissed us for lunch. As we walked away, he shouted: 'Oh, by the way, never make your players run laps of the field before they train or it will be a

waste of your time and theirs. See you after lunch.'

It was a lesson in coaching I have never forgotten.

The lesson I learned all those years ago is one that I would like to pass on to every player and coach of the game. Few coaching courses actually spend any real quality time with coaches telling them how to set out a warm-up. It is often only when a new coach has experiences of working with highly knowledgeable peers or with a high quality coach in their playing career, that they realize how important a warm-up actually is.

COMMON ERRORS

There are many ways to complete a warm-up with your team but you should not solely rely on your own personal experience on how to do your team's warm-up. A teaching friend of mine says that even history changes and if you rely on your own time as a player when it comes to the warm-up, there is a better than even chance you will be about fifteen years out of date.

Do you, as a coach, do any of these?

- Send the players on a run and when they get back ask them to do a little bit of stretching?
- Use the same warm-up for every session?

- Use warm-ups you have seen in other sports that have no link to rugby?
- Allow players to play touch before the session starts?
- Allow players to kick who never kick in matches (especially at posts!)?

If you do, you are not alone. Supervised, task-specific warm-ups are key to aiding your players not just for now but also for their long-term future health. Things that were common twenty years ago are still seen today but sports coaching has moved forward dramatically and preparing your players for the rugby game is now just as important as the actual playing of the game.

So what's the correct way to do a warm-up? Do I need a specialist to help me? Warm-ups are a very weighty subject and there are hugely qualified people who have written award-winning books and videos who could give you a better treatise on the warm-up than myself. However, if you look at the warm-up in a more thoughtful way, you can change the process without having to be a world-class expert.

INTENSITY

Figuring out the best way to approach the warm-up is usually based on what resources you have available. When you first start coaching, you put some drills or activities together and call it a training session. Trust me, every coach has done that at one point in his or her early career; there is nothing to be ashamed of in that.

At a normal club training session, the players' mindset when they arrive is not at game pace intensity. It's okay for you as the coach to tell the players that they have a problem in a certain area of the game but unless you can repeat the intensity of match play, they

will not see what you have seen. The players need to experience match-like pressure to show them what you saw and then provide them with preventative measures that can aid them in their next competitive fixture.

Some of the more experienced players will be honest enough to admit that there is an issue, and will have identified it themselves on match day but it's the egotistical and the talent-blind you have to convince. (I know you could film it and show it to them but most sessions of amateur teams are field-based and only rarely get a chance to go indoors.)

So how can you make a game mistake repeatable in training? The training session has to be as close to game intensity/pressure as possible before you can present your players with strategies to combat them. To get to that intensity, you have to complete a warm-up that will get the players to that point.

NON-CONTACT SESSIONS

Although it might seem a little simplistic, I cannot stress enough how important it is to focus on the body movements of your players. If you are doing a non-contact warm-up for handling for example, the upper body needs a little more concentration especially on the way the arms swing across the body. As you run in the warm-up, replicate the passing movement, even without the ball in the hands, and possibly include some evasion steps to the left and right that you wish your players to complete during the exercise.

Also, don't be afraid to have non-opposed passing exercises as part of your warm-up. Remember, you are building the session to reach a game intensity outcome and there is no time limit to a warm-up. If you want low-intensity stuff to be useful, work on technique before you get to the main event. Take your time: it's a process, not a quick fix.

Also, a warm-up is a great opportunity to really hone in on the technicalities of the skills you wish to explore. You haven't reached game intensity yet so you can just drop a few pointers in as they begin passing, running, etc. There is never a bad moment for a five-second coaching point.

In a non-contact session, you are trying to place mental pressure, in minimal space, onto the players so develop the session's structure accordingly. By working on movement and passing in the warm up, you have signalled to the players' mind and body that there will be no physicality in the session and reinforced that you want thoughtful solutions to the challenges you have placed in front of them without the danger of getting 'smashed' in a tackle. (Ideally of course you want thoughtful solutions at all times, but one step at a time ….)

CONTACT SESSIONS

If your team's issue is in the contact area, for example, simply getting them to smash into each other is not going to bring you the outcome you required – not if you want to have any control over your learning environment. At the start of the session, you must begin by changing their mindset that tonight's training session is going to be on this area. You can say it, but nothing sets a mindset for contact than a controlled, competitive warm-up. It sets the juices flowing.

1 vs. 1 or 2 vs. 1 physical activities will allow the players to get their 'game face' on while you are able to build the players to a point where you believe they are close to match intensity. If you want competition at the end, signal it in the warm-up and build slowly. The length of these 1 vs. 1s or 2 vs. 1s depends on whether the groups are finding the exercise too easy or too hard. You don't want anyone

standing around so when creating the competition, make sure everyone is paired with someone of his or her own position or of similar build. This will make the contests as competitive as possible.

As with non-contact, there is no time limit to warm-up so if you want to stay with 1 vs. 1 work, then stay with it. My advice here would be to ensure that each group of players has a ball to look after while they are in competition with each other – it's that way in the game so why not have that competition at all times?

MATCH WARM-UPS

Having spent all of those hours working with the players on set pieces, handling, breakdowns and so on, you turn up on game day, do a warm-up that bears no relation to the game you wish to play and subsequently get beaten.

As the coach, you instinctively know how your team plays. More experienced coaches will have completed a player audit and fashioned a team style based around the findings. Once you know what you wish to do to win the game, you should create a warm-up that prepares your players to meet that style.

If you feel that winning quick ball is key to your success, then rehearse your breakdown technique in the warm-up. Alternatively, if you think you have a chance of beating the opposition by running the ball wide, then practise that.

Note: change your warm-ups every month or so. You are looking for the warm-up to prepare the players' mind and body for game play but if they simply go through the motions having seen your warm-up a million times before, they will not get to where you need them. They will switch off, distract others and generally tune out.

SPRINT RELAYS

The difficulty with running sprint sessions is trying to make sure everyone puts in an equal amount of effort while also avoiding occasions when players can be seen to be running at half speed to preserve energy for later in the session. Try this drill to ensure all parties put their full effort in while working with peers in a similar position to theirs.

How it works

Fig. 1.1 At various points around the field, place marker cones as start/finish lines. The length of those sprints depends on what distances you wish your players to participate in at that time of the season. Place a team of sprinters at each marker cone – each team is made up of players in a similar position. This allows each to gauge where they are on the pecking order when compared to their peers. At one of the marker cones, place two teams.

Fig. 1.2 The coach starts the session but every sprint after this is started by the first player to arrive at the finish line for that particular sprint – i.e. they start the team waiting to go. The session is completed when every player gets back to where they started.

In our example, team F starts team A. The first arriving player from team A finishes, they start team B's sprint, and so on.

Fig. 1.1

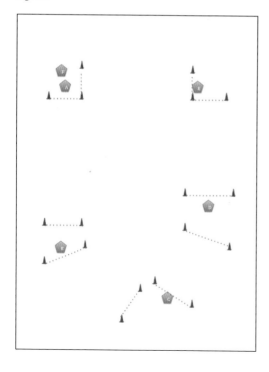

Fig. 1.2

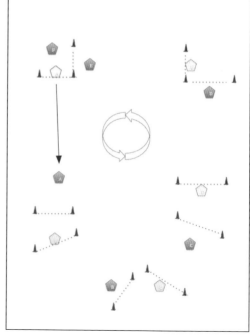

LEG AND LOWER BACK WARM-UP FOR RUCKING

If you are asking players to get lower when clearing out a ruck, it would help if the muscles they are being asked to use were ready to go when you made that point to them later in the session. This simple activity allows the players a little fun but also really gets the muscles working.

How it works

Fig. 1.3 Three players working together, with one shield working between the try line and the 22m line.

Fig. 1.4 Player 1 puts his hands on the shield and pushes it to the 22m where player 2 will push the shield to player 3 and so on.

Note: as the players become more fatigued, they will have the urge to raise their body height, resulting in the shield not moving forward.

Fig. 1.3

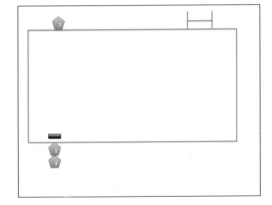

Fig. 1.4

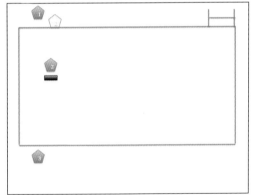

PHYSICAL INTENSITY

This drill really gets the blood flowing and adds a little aggressive competition prior to a physical contact session.

How it works
Fig. 1.5 In a 10m × 10m square, four players stand in a circle with a fifth player in the middle. The four players on the outside bind as tightly together as they can around the middle player they are not allowed to bind onto the middle player. The middle player must have their arms directly above their head. On the coach's call, the middle player has fifteen seconds to escape the circle.

Fig. 1.6 If the middle player succeeds, his teammates must complete a punishment task (push-ups, etc.). If the middle player is unsuccessful, his four team mates lie on the floor and the middle player has thirty seconds to drag them out of the square or receive a further punishment exercise.

Fig. 1.5

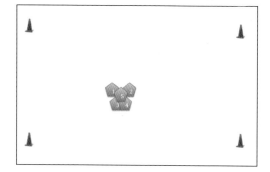

Fig. 1.6

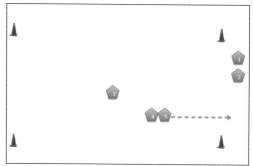

PRE-MATCH WARM-UPS

After many, many hours of practice, with highly planned training sessions, you arrive at the day of the match and you suddenly find that your team is simply lacklustre. Of course there are a hundred reasons why this might have happened but one of the most common is that your warm-up hasn't allowed the players to mentally prepare for the rigours ahead. Here, I show you a different way of thinking about the pre-match warm up.

How it works
On match day, you will have the exclusive use of half the field – use it all.

Fig. 1.7   Divide your half of the field into three distinct areas:

Area 1 – handling
Area 2 – contact
Area 3 – defence

It is at your discretion what you wish to complete in each of these areas and for how long but I always like to do my defence work close to our try line as it plants the seed that when we get into this position, hard work must follow.

Fig. 1.7

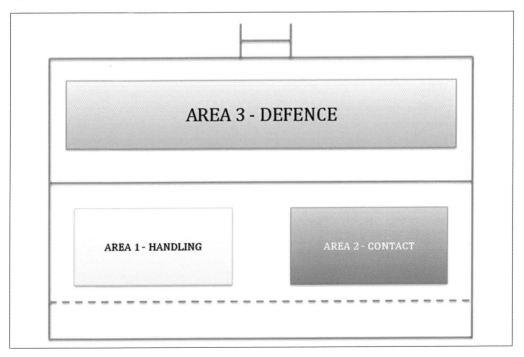

RUCK WARM-UP ON HARD GROUND

To develop your team's contact skills when the ground is at its hardest is a difficult thing to do. In parts of the world where the sun always shines, hard ground is a fact of life; however, there is a way to warm up for contact without throwing yourself on the ground. This activity allows a degree of contact to occur but also allows your players relative safety when falling to the ground.

How it works

Fig. 1.0 Place a number of shields on the ground in two lines. Players work in pairs.

Fig. 1.9 Player 1 runs with a ball to a shield on the floor and falls, with correct technique, onto it. Once on the ground, they pop the ball up to player 2, who runs over player 1 and falls onto the next shield. Player 1, by this time, is back on their feet ready to take the ball from player 2. The drill is a continuous one until all of the shields have been negotiated.

Fig. 1.8

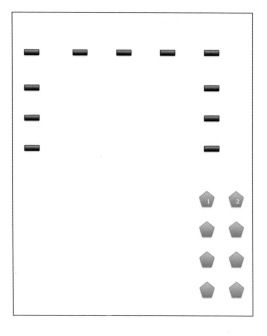

Fig. 1.9

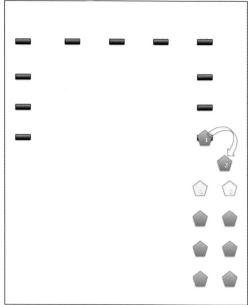

USE THE FIELD (1): AEROBIC RUNS

Sometimes young coaches forget that the field has markings on it that can be used in very useful ways to judge many different things about your players. The next few drills look at innovative ways you can use your rugby field as a fitness asset. All of them will allow you as the coach to meet the needs of your players while also having them work where you can see them all – when tiredness comes, some can try to hide!

How it works

Fig. 1.10 Starting on the try line, each player must run to each full line and back. You can set a time for each player position; for example the props do not have the same time as the wingers.

Fig. 1.10

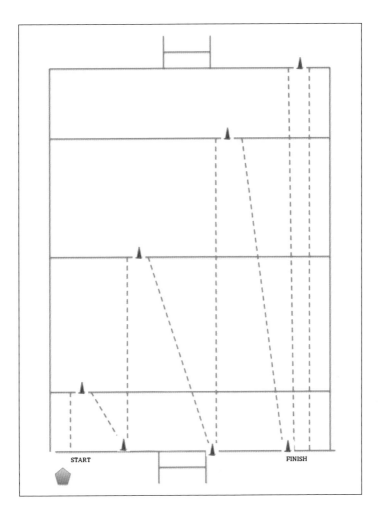

USE THE FIELD (2): AEROBIC INTERVAL TRAINING

Interval training is a series of activities that are not of the same intensity at all times. In this example, it is sprints interspersed with jogging and walking rest periods. This can help your team prepare for the season as the game of rugby isn't played at full intensity at all times but when speed or aggression is required, it would help if the body was already adapted and adjusted to that style by completing tasks such as these.

How it works
Fig. 1.11 Using the markings on the field as start or finish lines, each player starts at one corner and follows the directives that you set out. In this particular example: walk to 22m, jog from 22m to try line, sprint across the width of the field and repeat on the other side. You can of course use variations or different types of interval training for each playing position.

Fig. 1.11

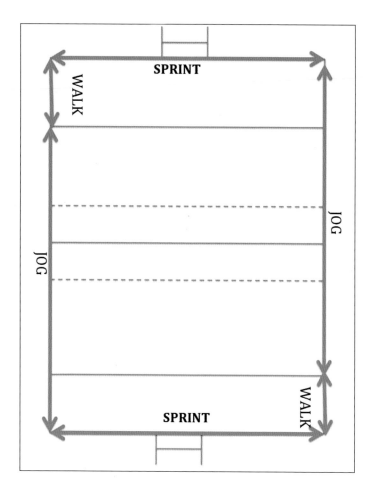

USE THE FIELD (3): CHASE SPRINTS

Competition in training is essential in creating a successful rugby programme so this drill pits two players of equal ability to chase each other down over a shortened course.

How it works
Fig. 1.12   Have player 1 (the 'fox') stand on the corner of the 'dead ball' area of your field. Have player 2 (the 'rabbit') stand on the corner of the field directly in front of them.
On the coach's call, the rabbit sprints to the 22m flag diagonally across from them, round the flag and runs along the 22m line to the finish. The fox has to catch the rabbit.

Note: never underestimate how competitive your players are with each other; it is essential that you pair players of near-equal ability to get the best out of this activity.

Fig. 1.12

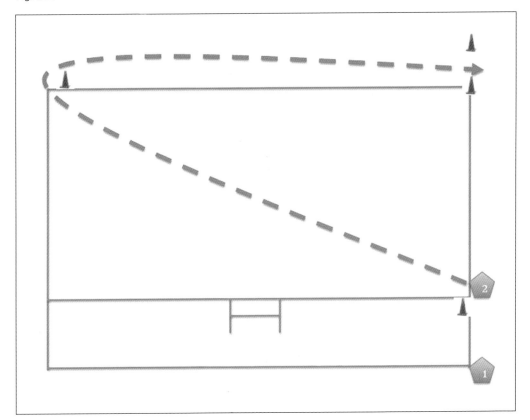

USE THE FIELD (4): STAGGERED SPRINTS

The one area that concerns most front five players is that when it comes to fitness, the fastest players get the most rest. If you think about it logically, a prop doesn't have to sprint as far as a winger might in a match, so why make them complete the same sprints in training?

Also, if you make every player run 100m, the players who finish first will be recovering while many of the team are still working. Here is a drill that allows you to get everyone working at the same intensity level with each receiving equal recovery periods before continuing.

How it works

Fig. 1.13 Depending on which position each player plays, decide which lines they sprint between. In this example, all players must sprint to the try line, but each position starts on a different line to ensure that all players finish the sprints at the same time. The props start on the 10m line closest to the finish line. The second row start on the half-way line. The back row start on the furthest away 10m line. The half backs (9s and 10s) and centres start on the far 22m line. The wingers and full backs start on the far try line. On the coach's call, each player sprints at their fullest to the try line. It may take a little 'promotion' to sort out but what you are looking for is a genuine race to the try line with each player having a realistic chance of winning.

Note: if you feel a player is finishing significantly further ahead than the rest of his group, 'promote' them into another team further back. At first they will not be pleased, but secretly they will be happy you have noticed their individual abilities.

Fig. 1.13

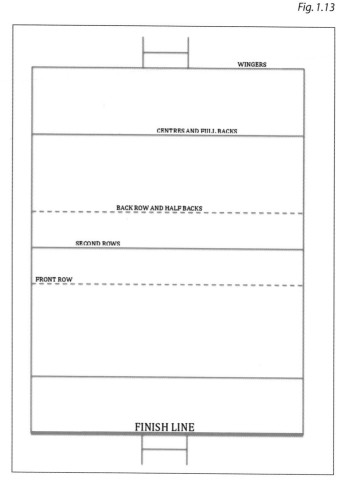

USE THE FIELD (5): DYNAMIC WARM-UP CHANNELS

One of the newest innovations in warm-up over the last twenty years has been the growth of 'dynamic stretching'. Much has been written on the subject of dynamic stretching and there are a number of YouTube clips showing what should be done to complete it correctly. However, this drill gets the best use out of it for your team whilst ensuring that they are constantly working.

How it works
Fig. 1.14 Mark out two channels, one of which starts under the posts. Working with teams of four, begin the dynamic stretching activity, working down one channel.

At the end of the channel, all four players stop, ensure they are all in a line and then 'shuffle' into the next channel as a line. Once in the other channel, they turn around, and work back to the start again while completing the same activity they completed in the previous channel.

Fig. 1.14

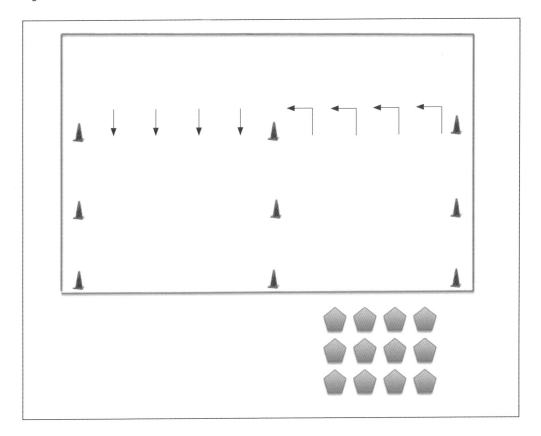

CHAPTER 2 – PASSING

This chapter contains the following drills designed to develop skills in passing.

Basic Passing (1)

Basic Passing: Balance

Basic Passing (2)

Basic Passing: Fatigue

Basic Passing (3)

High Intensity Passing: Fatigue

High Pressure Passing: Space

Scrum Half Passing

Continuous Reaction Drill for 10s

Channel Running

Clearing Pass (1)

Clearing Pass (2)

Clearing Pass: Messy Ball

Running from Depth (1)

Running from Depth (2)

Running from Depth (3)

Three vs. Two

Running from Depth (4)

Starting the Scan

Random Attack and Defence

Attack the Space (1)

Attack the Space (2)

Beat the Full Back

Reaction and Communication

The 'No-Look' Pass

High Intensity Drill: Fatigue

Loop Attack

CHAPTER 2

Passing

Although one of the key basic skills of the rugby game, passing is often assumed as a player skill rather than one that needs upgrading regularly in training sessions. There is a very famous story of an England coach completing a tackling training session in the mid-1990s and one of the players admitting to him that he hadn't been taught tackle technique since he was seven years old, as all coaches he had played for assumed he could do it as a professional rugby player. How often do you check that all of your players can actually pass correctly off both the left and right hand?

The key factors of a pass are among the very first things coaches are tasked to teach but what is often forgotten as players mature is how important it is to return to the skill and how it is executed under pressure.

Passing is often rushed, inaccurate or poorly completed simply as a result of misreading the defence but we as coaches do not return to that skill as often as we should. Throughout this book I stress the fact that players must be asked to use their skills with opposition, building to the point where they become comfortable under pressure and are able to make positive, insightful decisions in the most hectic of conditions.

That being said, the reason why most teams cannot reach the point in the defence where they are able to exploit a space is often down to an inability to pass the ball in front of the receiver who runs onto the ball. A well-placed pass in front of a receiver will allow the ball to reach its target before the defence can slide across and fill the break in their defence.

While looking at these passing drills, keep in mind how often your players place the ball in front of the receiver, allowing them to catch the ball and look at the defender with only a small adjustment of the head. Successful completion of the drill may be wholesale issues with your team's overall skill levels but don't throw all of your hard work out of the window. Often it can be something so simple that even the best coaches can miss it so I would urge you to run a simple 'passing the ball' exercise with your team and see where they stand when tasked with a simple activity.

The reason that some of your players may be unable to complete the drill isn't necessarily that they do not see the solution; it may be they do not possess the passing ability to complete it.

BASIC PASSING (1)

This drill is designed to ensure that players can pass left/right but run straight.

How it works
Fig. 2.1   In groups of three, players pass along the line but must stay running forward and within the channel created by the lines/cones. This activity allows the coach to see which players have difficulty passing; it stops attack 'drift' that closes down space out wide; and it allows the coach to see which players need a little help.

To increase difficulty
- Increase distances between the passes.
- Increase the speed of the run.
- Put a time limit on the number of passes that need to be made to ensure everyone gets their hands on the ball.
- Reduce the width of the running channel.

Fig. 2.1

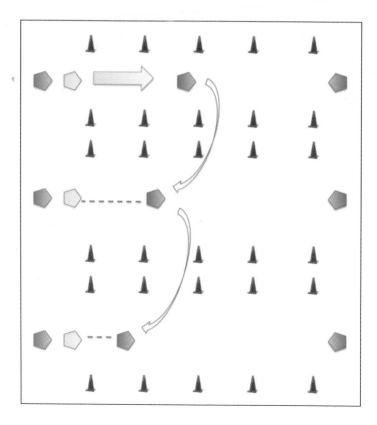

BASIC PASSING: BALANCE

Despite what many coaching manuals will tell you, you cannot always determine which foot is placed forward when you pass a ball to a colleague. This drill gets the players to isolate their upper body and arms to make passes without having any assistance from the lower body.

How it works
Have two players facing each other with a ball, one of whom is on one leg, 10 metres away.

Fig. 2.2   Player 1 passes the ball to player 2 (on one leg) who takes a pass and immediately passes back. Player 2 then bounces 90 degrees to the left and takes another pass – immediately passing it back.

Fig. 2.3   When player 2's back is to his partner, he needs to receive one pass on the right side, pass it back and then one on the left side, pass it back, then bounce 90 degrees again. The player on one leg keeps moving 90 degrees until they have completed two full turns (twelve passes); then change to their other leg and continue. Then change partners.

Note: the side the ball is caught on is the side the ball must be passed back, i.e. the ball caught by Player 2 on the right hand side must be passed back from that side.

To increase difficulty
■ Increase distances between player 1 and player 2.
■ Have player 2 bend their knees before passing the ball back.

Fig. 2.2

Fig. 2.3

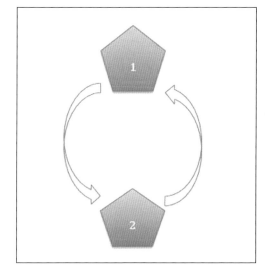

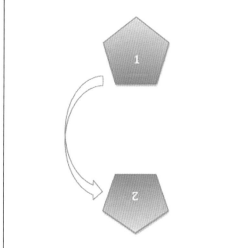

BASIC PASSING (2)

This activity is designed to help the coach identify players who have difficulty passing on one side. When running this activity, it is more difficult to complete for everyone than it first appears, but with perseverance it can significantly aid the players to achieve more complex passing tasks later in their development.

How it works
Fig. 2.4 Create a 10m × 10m box with cones. Place one player at each corner facing inwards. Pass the ball in any direction using the power in the hands only. Often, players use their lower body, core and a 'step' towards the intended receiver to achieve a pass off a weaker side. By insisting players must remain in one place and simply use their hands you will be able to see who needs some assistance before moving on to more complex passing activities. This activity begins the learning path for the player to run straight and not drift towards the player they are passing to.

To increase difficulty
- Increase the size of the box.
- Make the players pass whilst on their knees.
- Pass with one foot off the floor, which ensures strength in the arms are the reason for success (the player will fall over if they use any other movement of their body to make the pass).

Fig. 2.4

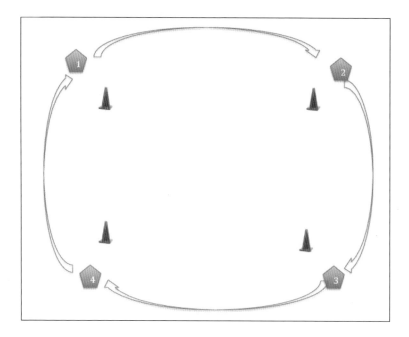

BASIC PASSING: FATIGUE

Most players can pass without any pressure. What makes passes inaccurate is increasing the pressure in several match-related ways such as, in this case, making the players pass whilst fatigued.

How it works
This is a simple pass and follow game with added pressure.

Fig. 2.5 Four players stand at four cones with one ball (10m × 10m area). Player 1 passes the ball to player 2 but runs to the cone where player 2 is standing.

Fig. 2.6 Upon reaching player 2's cone, they perform one push-up and return to their own cone ready to receive the next pass.

To increase difficulty
- Increase the distance between the cones.
- Have two teams competing against the clock – winners are the team with the most successful passes completed.
- Ask the players to perform more activities without the ball – forward roll and a push-up, two push-ups and a star jump, etc.

Fig. 2.5

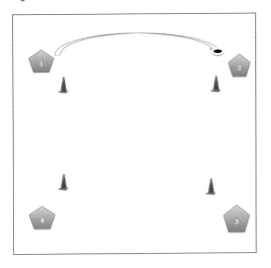

Fig. 2.6

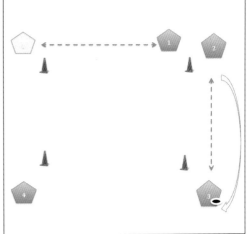

BASIC PASSING (3)

Following on from the previous activity, this activity stresses even more the requirement for ambitious rugby players to be able to pass a ball by using just their upper body and forearms.

How it works
Work in groups of three with a ball. One player lies on their back; the remaining two players stand about 2 metres away, about level with the player's chest. Standing player 1 passes the ball to the hands of the lying player; the lying player has to make the pass using their forearms only to standing player 2. Player 2 passes the ball back immediately and the activity continues.

Fig. 2.7 Once accuracy is achieved, ask the two standing players to take one step backwards, then continue.

Fig. 2.8 Keep stepping backwards until the lying player has reached their limit and then swap over.

Note: the lying player will sometimes begin to make 'netball-type' chest passes where they push the ball to the side instead of passing the ball correctly. They will do this as this is the easiest pass to make whilst lying on the floor but it doesn't aid their rugby passing development. Ensure at all times the correct pass type is made.

To increase difficulty
- The middle player is in a seated position.
- The middle player sits cross-legged which makes the player pass the ball closer to their chest.

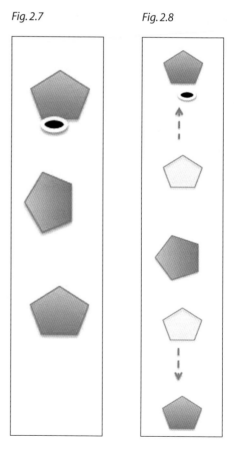

Fig. 2.7   *Fig. 2.8*

HIGH-INTENSITY PASSING: FATIGUE

Key skills of rugby need to be repeated often and under pressure. This drill puts the pressure on the players mentally while allowing the coach to watch their passing technique. This drill can be performed by your entire squad at one time and is restricted by how much rest you wish them to have – the larger the numbers, the longer the rest.

How it works
Using the 22m area as length, place cones 20m in from touch. To begin, get players A to D to pass a ball as quickly as possible while running across the area.

Fig. 2.9 Once the ball gets to the other side, all four players (A, B, C and D) must run around the outside of the area and back to their original starting line. Player D gives the ball to player H and that line returns the ball across the area to the next waiting line.

Fig. 2.10 After a set amount of time, make the players pass to the left.

To increase difficulty
■ Increase the distance each player has to pass.
■ Introduce more rugby balls to the activity.

Fig. 2.9

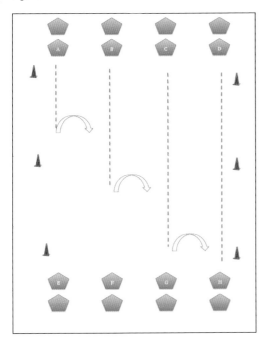

Fig. 2.10

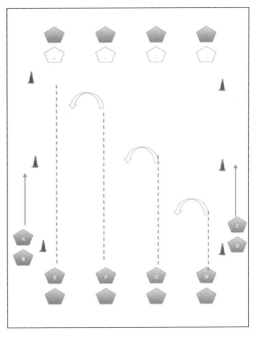

HIGH-PRESSURE PASSING: SPACE

This activity is designed for players to use not only their passing skills but also their judgment on when to pass and to use their footwork to evade the other people in the group to ensure the pass is made successfully.

How it works

Fig. 2.11 Each team of four runs across to the other side of the 20m × 20m box to reach the other side – they must ensure that each member of their team passes/receives a ball before reaching the other side of the grid.

Fig. 2.11

Fig. 2.12 Upon reaching the other side, each team runs around a cone and realigns on the side of the grid directly to their right.

Fig. 2.13 Having gone around the cone, the ball carrier stands close to that cone while their team reposition themselves for the next run across the grid.

To increase difficulty
■ As the team make three passes crossing the grid, give a target number of passes to be made in a set time limit, e.g. twenty-one passes in two minutes.

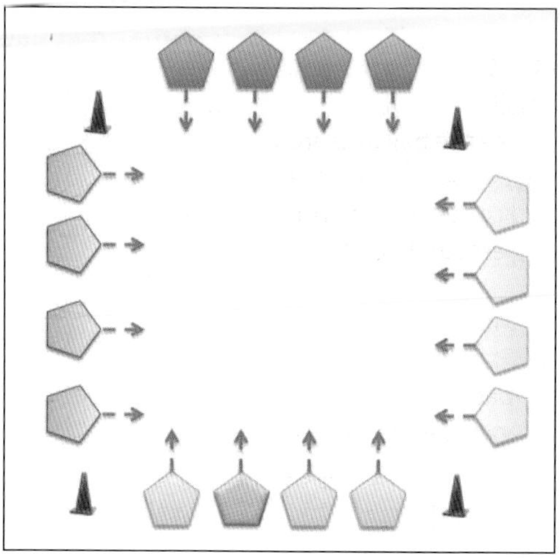

Fig. 2.12

Fig. 2.13

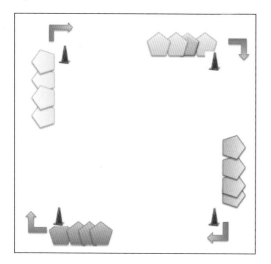

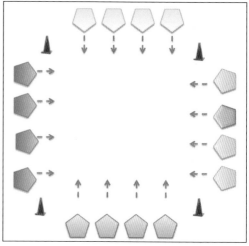

SCRUM HALF PASSING

This drill is designed for you to see your scrum half pass off both hands while giving him a moving target to work with. It also allows you to see which players can catch a ball and run while still managing to run straight.

How it works

Fig. 2.14   Place marker cones in channels of about 1m width. Leave a 5m gap in the cones at the mid-way point for a player to sidestep into the next channel. There should be approximately 20ms between each channel. In the middle are two areas used to place the balls into. There should be enough balls for every player to receive a pass.

Fig. 2.15   As each player runs, alternating between left and right channels, the 9 passes a ball to each player from area 1. The ball carrier reaches the end of that channel, sidesteps and places the ball into area 2 and continues the run into the other channel. In our example, player 1 takes a pass from 9 in channel 1. They then sidestep into the middle to place the ball into area 2 and continue their run into channel 2. When all passes have been made, 9 runs to next area and players run from the other direction.

To increase difficulty

■ Start the players off more quickly so the 9 has to make left and right passes at a much faster pace.
■ Increase the distance the 9 has to pass.

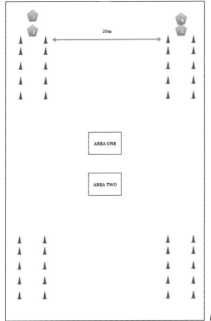

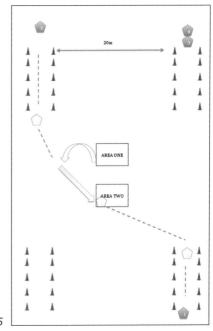

Fig. 2.14 *Fig. 2.15*

CONTINUOUS REACTION DRILL FOR 10s

As coaches, we ask an awful lot of our number 10s but do we actually prepare them properly to make correct passing decisions when we need them to? Here is a drill to see if your players need work on making decisions under pressure and begins to look at the use of 'dummy' runners.

How it works
Fig. 2.16   A scrum half, a 10 and support runner (S2) stands behind S1. Two defenders stand near the three spaces.

Fig. 2.17   As soon as the scrum half touches the ball, the two defenders run at two of the spaces. The 10 then has to decide which pass needs to be made to exploit the space left behind. Once completed – success or failure – the attack move to the end of the channel and once the defenders reset themselves, the drill begins again.

Options for 10
- Keep the ball as defenders take spaces two and three.
- Miss pass to S2, who runs wide.
- Pass to S1.
- Pass behind S1 to dummy runner S2 (be careful not to block defender).

Fig. 2.16

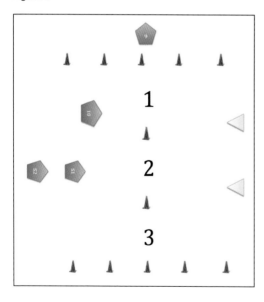

Fig. 2.17

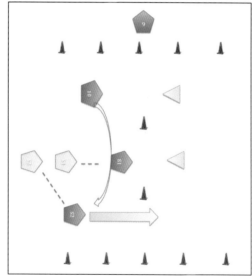

CHANNEL RUNNING

Running straight when in possession of the ball ensures the space your team mates have is not taken away from them. However, there are moments in matches when the ball carrier needs to evade a defender, hence closing the space for a potential receiver. This activity is designed to look at the movement of the ball carrier and how to react accordingly.

How it works
Create four channels, each about 2–10m wide (depending on the skill of the participants). One player stands in each channel with two defenders at the far end.

Fig. 2.18 A person acting as scrum half makes a pass to one of the channels. The two defenders close to make a touch tackle on the ball carrier. The ball carrier is allowed to leave their channel but once they do, another player must step into that channel – only one player per channel is allowed.

Fig. 2.19 In the example shown, SH passes the ball to player 1. Player 1 (to try to evade defender 1) steps into another channel. Player 1 and player 2 are now in the same channel. Player 2 steps into a free channel; player 1 has player 2 and player 3 to pass to.

To increase difficulty
- Increase the number of defenders.
- Increase the space of each channel to make the passing more challenging.
- Decrease the distance between the attack and defence.

Fig. 2.18

Fig. 2.19

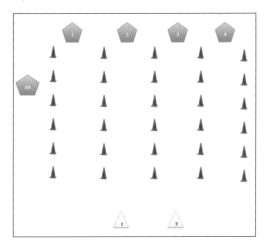

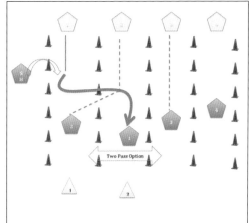

CLEARING PASS (1)

Although the best passer from the back of a ruck, maul, scrum or line-out is the scrum half, it is unrealistic to believe that the 9 will be at every breakdown. This activity is a simple one that allows many people to practise a pass from a ruck (in this instance) and allows players to receive a pass.

How it works

Fig. 2.20 Players in two lines work in pairs,

Fig. 2.20

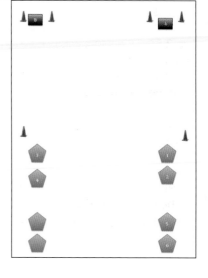

Fig. 2.21 Player 1 takes a ball up to shield A lying on the floor in front of them and places it just in front of it – then they step over. Player 2 follows player 1 and when the ball is placed, player 2 passes the ball to player 3 (players 1 and 2 return to the start).

Fig. 2.22 Player 3 places the ball in front of Shield B, which player 4 passes to player 5. The process repeats.

To increase difficulty
- Have player 1 roll the ball back towards player 2 (simple at first but then roll the ball end over end).
- Player 1 falls on the tackle shield and presents as a ruck ball presentation.
- Player 1 can pass the ball to player 2 over their head.
- Have each pair run to the opposite team after running over the shield.

Fig. 2.21

Fig. 2.22

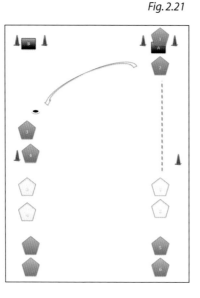

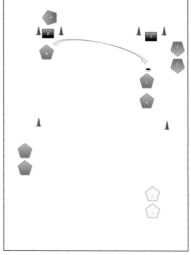

CLEARING PASS (2)

How it works

Fig. 2.23   Make a grid 30m × 30m. Inside this grid, make another grid 5m × 5m. Place four balls on the inside grid and evenly spread your players between the cones on the outside grid. Players 1–4 run into the middle and place the ball at the cone directly in front of them.

Fig. 2.24   They move to the cone on their right.

Fig. 2.25   They then make a clearing pass to the front player who is directly in line with this new cone. The player then joins that team and the new ball carriers continue the process.

To increase difficulty
- Reverse direction.
- Instead of running to next cone, run to the cone opposite their line (run two cones).
- When all four reach the middle, they each pop the ball in the air and run to the next ball before it bounces, then make the pass.

Fig. 2.23

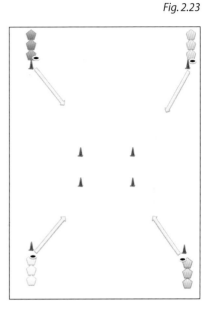

Fig. 2.24

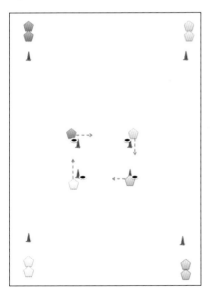

Fig. 2.25

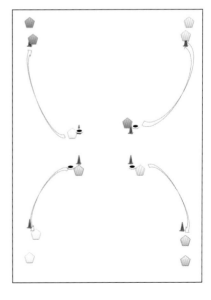

CLEARING PASS: MESSY BALL

As any scrum half will tell you, as much as coaches try to teach the players to give them clean ball (easy to reach and pass), sometimes the shape of the ball or other factors impact on the way the ball comes to scrum half before they can pass it onwards. This drill is a simple way to train your scrum half to react to 'messy' ball.

How it works
Fig. 2.26   Have one player with a ball kneeling next to a goal post (without padding). The scrum half stands 2m away from this goal post. The rest of the back line stands in two lines 15m away from the scrum half.

Fig. 2.27   The kneeling player throws the ball at the post and the scrum half has to chase and pass the ball to one of the receivers in the lines. That receiver returns the ball to the kneeling player.

To increase difficulty
■ Once the ball has hit the post, the coach decides which player gets the ball.

Fig. 2.26

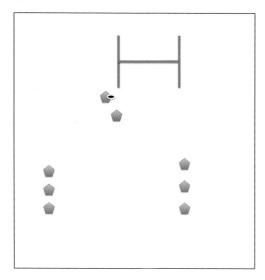

Fig. 2.27

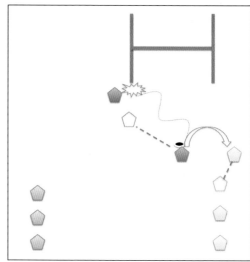

RUNNING FROM DEPTH (1)

Teaching players to delay their run in support of the ball carrier is an issue at all levels of the game. This activity forces the players to run around a pre-determined cone which gives the coach the chance to show each player how effective running from depth can be – both in options available and impact speed on catching the ball at pace.

How it works
Fig. 2.28   Place four cones at either end of a 20m channel, 3m apart, across the start and finish line to create channels.

Fig. 2.29   On your call, the three attackers run around their designated cones and attack. The defender runs the opposite way and has the freedom to defend in any way they wish. Have three attackers run around the cones as shown with one defender running around their cone.

To increase difficulty
- Once the players become more successful, add a second defender.
- Decrease the time.
- Remove the need for the attackers to run around their cones.

Fig. 2.28

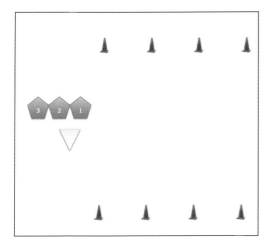

Fig. 2.29

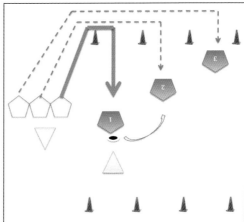

RUNNING FROM DEPTH (2)

Although the previous activity does serve a very valuable purpose in teaching the basics of the draw and pass, in match play, defenders rarely all come from one side – they usually have to be dealt with from multiple directions and you rarely outnumber them three to one. This activity begins the process of game-related practice for attack play.

How it works
Fig. 2.30   Place six cones to create a 20m channel. On this occasion, place a defender at either side of the channel.

Fig. 2.31   On your call, the three attackers run around the nearest cone and attack. Both defenders run to their nearest cone and defend the channel.

To increase difficulty
■ Place a time limit for the attack to score their try.

Fig. 2.30

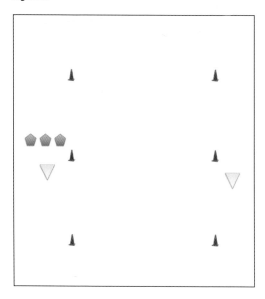

Fig. 2.31

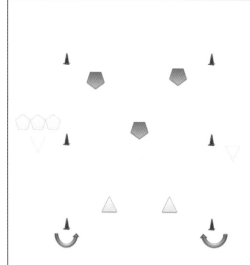

RUNNING FROM DEPTH (3)

Having dealt with the defence coming from differing angles, to make it as game-realistic as possible, this activity adds another defender but this time he chases the three attackers up the channel.

How it works
Fig. 2.32   Place six cones to create a 20m × 12m channel. In addition to the two defenders on either side of the channel, a third defender stands next to the three attackers.

On your call, the three attackers run around the nearest cone and attack. Both defenders run to their nearest cone and defend the channel. Once the three attackers enter the channel, the third defender chases them, simulating a recovering defender.

To increase difficulty
■   Allow full contact to take place.
■   Allow the third defender to chase a little earlier as the attackers become more proficient.

Fig. 2.32

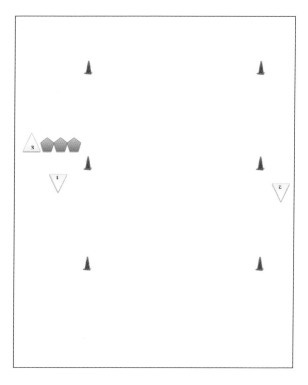

THREE vs. TWO

The holy grail of rugby is to find yourself in open space with a numerical advantage. However, we see so many teams who forget the basics of 3 vs. 2 and consequently fall down in its execution. What on the surface seems a very simple activity actually has many facets and solutions but the answer is usually based on what the defenders do in reaction to what your players do.

How it works
Five players (minimum), using a 30m × 20m channel. You throw the ball to one of them and they must beat the two defenders opposite to score.

Fig. 2.33 If you throw the ball to the player 1, defender 1 will run to the ball carrier leaving defender 2 to decide which one of attacker 2 and 3 to defend. It is this decision attacker A needs to look at before passing. Following a scan of the defence, the pass they make will be dependent on what they see defender 2 do (simple pass to attacker 1, or a miss pass to attacker 2).

Fig. 2.34 If you throw the ball to the middle (attacker 2), the defence then has to decide who must tackle the ball carrier and which of the two remaining attackers is an immediate threat. Following a scan of the defence, the support player that is unmarked, gets the ball.

To increase difficulty
■ Have the defenders come from different directions and not straight on.
■ Make the area wider – great activity for practising 7s.

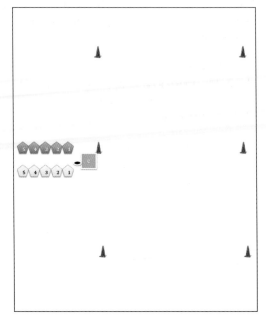

Fig. 2.33

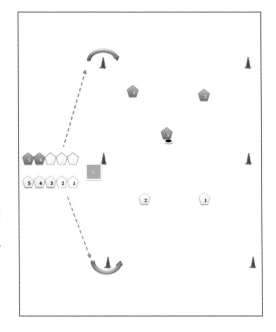

Fig. 2.34

RUNNING FROM DEPTH (4)

There are many occasions when a ball carrier has to make a decision to engage a defender or draw them away from a supporting runner before making a pass. This drill creates that situation for the ball carrier. It is a full contact drill.

How it works
Fig. 2.35 Four players stand 5m apart on the right hand side of a channel. In front of them are placed tackle tubes which they must run around. Further down the channel are three defenders situated 10m apart.

Fig. 2.36 On the coach's call, the players run around the tackle tubes and try to score at the far end of the channel. To begin with, the defenders can only move to the left and right to stop the attackers.

Fig. 2.35

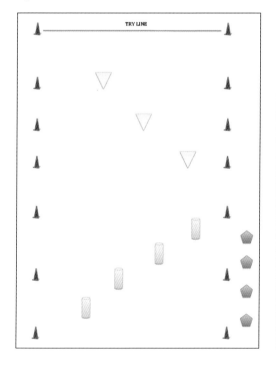

Fig. 2.36

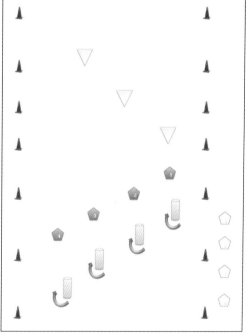

STARTING THE SCAN

In rugby play, the transition from an attacking to a defensive mindset needs to happen very quickly, especially in cases of turnover or counter-attacks. This activity allows you to work with your squad, giving them the opportunity to use those transition skills.

How it works
Fig. 2.37   Create a 20m × 15m channel. In the middle of one side have two lines of players with you in between, with a ball.

Figs. 2.38 and 2.39   You pass the ball to one team and three of them go around the cone and attack. The opposition team who did not get the ball automatically put two players in defence and they run around the cone to create a 3 vs. 2 game. Once the game is concluded, the players return to the opposite teams they departed from.

To increase difficulty
■ Place a time limit to complete the task.
■ Ask the third man in attack to complete one push-up before starting.

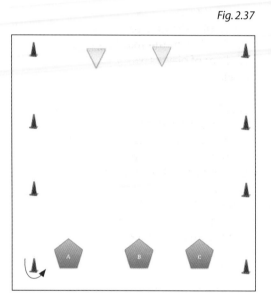
Fig. 2.37

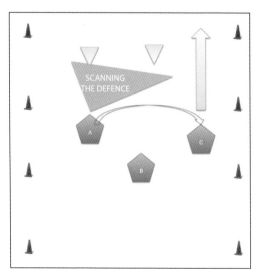
Fig. 2.38

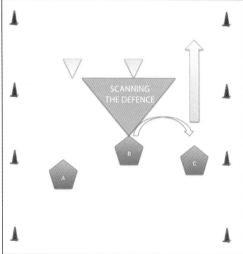
Fig. 2.39

RANDOM ATTACK AND DEFENCE

Having looked at transitioning from attack to defence, an expansion would be to look at what happens a little more closely. Once a line break has been made (following a successful 3 vs. 2), in match play there are also covering players to negotiate. This activity brings this home in a fun and energetic way.

Fig. 2.40

How it works

Fig. 2.40 Create two 20m × 15m channels side-by-side. In the middle of one side have two lines of players with you in between with a ball.

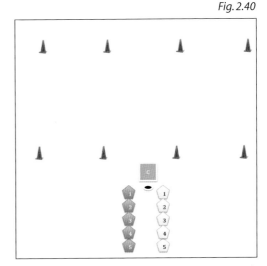

Figs. 2.41 and 2.42 You pass the ball to one team and three of them go around the cone and attack. The opposition team who did not get the ball automatically put two players in defence and they run around the cone to create a 3 vs. 2 game. This time, instead of the game finishing after the first 3 vs. 2, the game moves to the next channel with the all continuing their run to attack/defend once again.

Fig. 2.41

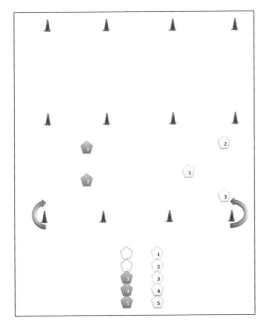

Fig. 2.42

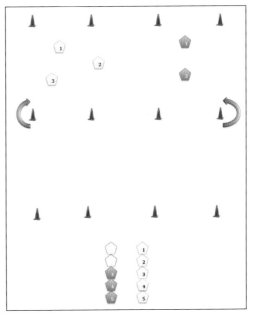

ATTACK THE SPACE (1)

Exploit the space
The ability of a ball carrier to look at the defence once they have the ball is a skill that needs to be learned and developed through activities such as these.

How it works
Fig. 2.43 Three attackers stand at the end of a 15m channel facing three 'gates'. Behind the gates are two defenders.

Fig. 2.44 When the scrum half (SH) passes the ball to attacker 1, the defenders step into a gate of their choosing leaving only one 'open' for a free attacker to run through. With effective communication from the attacker with the open gate, and good scanning by attacker 1, the ball can be quickly passed to attacker 3.

Fig. 2.43

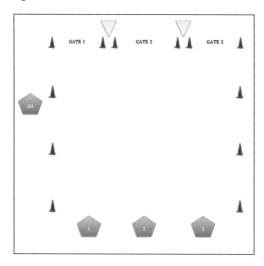

Fig. 2.44

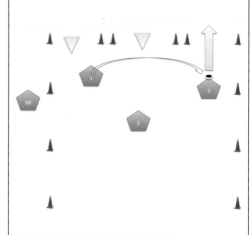

ATTACK THE SPACE (2)

Having looked to develop the ability of a ball carrier to look at the defence and pass to a free attacker, we now look at the need to sometimes preserve the space for others to exploit.

How it works
Fig. 2.45 Three attackers stand at the end of a 15m channel facing three 'gates'. Behind the gates are two defenders.

Fig. 2.46 When SH passes the ball to attacker 1, the defenders step into a gate of their choosing leaving only one 'open' for a free attacker to run through (in this instance, they step in gates 1 and 3. With effective communication from the attacker with the open gate, and good scanning by attacker 1, the ball can be quickly passed to attacker 3.

Fig. 2.47 If there is a space in gate 1, attacker 1 steps into defender 1, and switches with attacker 2.

To increase difficulty
■ Have the defenders step into the gates and then run forward.

Fig. 2.45

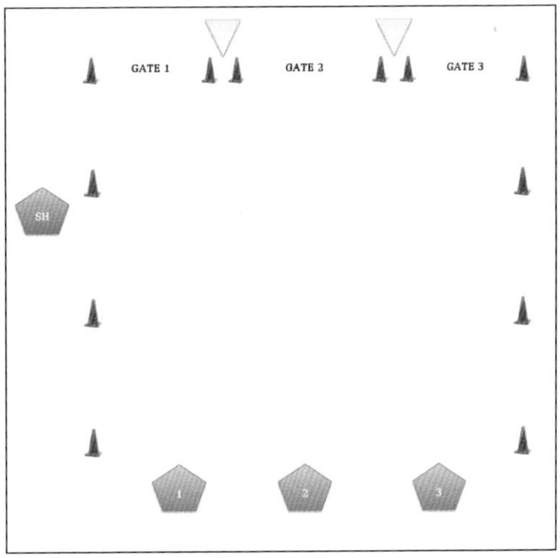

Fig. 2.46

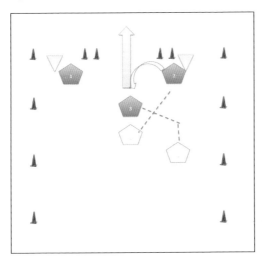

Fig. 2.47

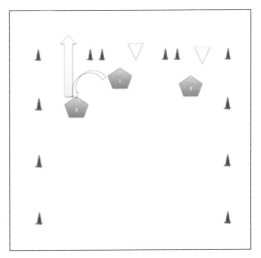

BEAT THE FULL BACK

In matches, your team will breach the defensive line at some point. However, most teams do not practise what happens after this occurs, so to aid your thoughts and planning post line break, here is an activity to get your point across to your team.

How it works
Figs 2.48, 2.49 and 2.50

Fig. 2.48

- Set up a 40m × 20m channel. You need a scrum half, four players and four defenders, different coloured cones and a ball. Four attackers run at three defenders and a full back. On your call, the three defenders fill three of five spaces available. Having passed the ball accurately, a ball carrier with a space in front will break the line. Then the two remaining players have to beat the full back using a pressurized 2 vs. 1 pass.

Note: the full back doesn't move forward until the line break has been made.

To increase difficulty
- Move the start line closer to the defenders, allowing less time for the players to see the space and call for the ball.
- Add a defender leaving one space – this will make the penetrating ball carrier have to beat the full back 1 on 1.
- Take the cones away for the defenders and allow much more freedom of movement with your attack.

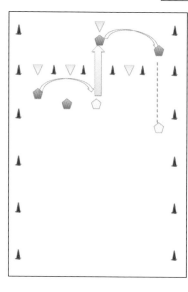
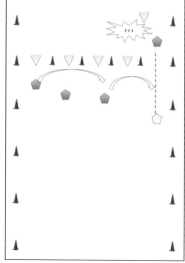

Figs. 2.49 and 2.50

REACTION AND COMMUNICATION

When a player has to turn and retrieve a ball, very often it is not until they turn and face back down the field that they know what their options are for the counter-attack. This drill allows two players to communicate while one has their back to a chasing defender.

How it works
Fig. 2.51   Two players stand half-way down a channel facing their own line. A defender stands on their own try line.

Fig. 2.52   The coach rolls a ball towards the attackers' line and both players chase. One player decides to retrieve the ball while the other should be looking back up the channel and telling the retriever what they are to do once they have the ball (keep it, pass it, how much time they have, etc.).

To increase difficulty
■   Have one attacker and the defender stand next to each other while the retriever stands half-way down. Will the chasing support player be able to effectively communicate from a distance?

Fig. 2.51

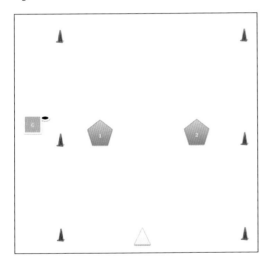

Fig. 2.52

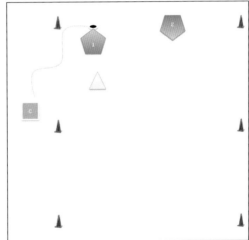

THE 'NO-LOOK' PASS

As your players grow in confidence and become more skillful, more recognition of what the defence is doing (as opposed to turning around to see who on your team is close to you) will need to be developed. Your support players will learn to communicate better and therefore an opportunity may arise for you to use a 'no-look' pass. Of course, this type of pass needs many, many hours of practice so to begin that journey, here is a simple drill.

How it works
Fig. 2.53 Ask four players to stand at each corner of a grid with one player standing in the middle. The two players in front have a ball each.

Fig. 2.54 One at a time, a ball is passed to the middle player and he must pass the ball to one of the players standing behind them in the grid without looking – all he hears is where they are standing. When the ball is received at the back of the grid, it is passed to the front again and the activity continues.

Note: a ball from the right hand side receiver must go to the right-hand side receiver and similarly on the left.

To increase difficulty
- Make the grid smaller so the passes happen faster.
- Make the grid larger so the passers have to put more effort in to make the distance required.

Fig. 2.53

Fig. 2.54

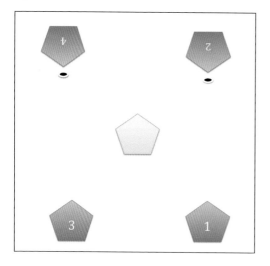

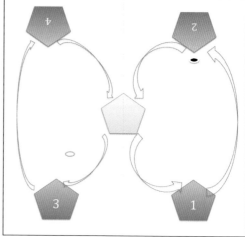

HIGH INTENSITY DRILL: FATIGUE

This activity can be completed against the clock while one team is working; their peers are watching them perform, which adds another type of pressure.

How it works
Fig. 2.55   Make two channels about 30m × 20m each. Four attackers line up in channel 1; two defenders stand at the end of channel 2.

Fig. 2.56   On the coach's call, the attackers make three passes while getting to the top of channel 1. As they turn into channel 2, the two defenders run up the channel and prevent the team from scoring. Success or failure, the ball is retrieved and the attackers return to channel 1 and the activity begins again.

To increase difficulty
■ Add another defender.
■ Add a punishment exercise to complete once the time limit has expired based on the number of dropped passes.

Fig. 2.55

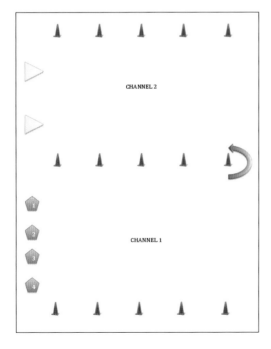

Fig. 2.56

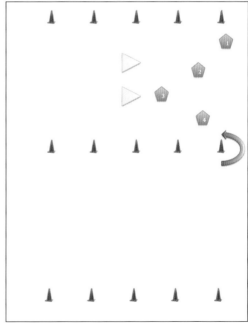

LOOP ATTACK

Due to significant improvements in defensive organization over recent years, the loop has fallen out of favour somewhat as teams move more and more to multiple phases rather than pulling a defence laterally before attacking the line. However, loops occur naturally in the game and aren't often planned so why not work on what is required just in case it happens to your team.

How it works
Fig. 2.57   Create a 30m × 20m channel. Three players attack three tackle tubes. SH starts the game.

Fig. 2.58   Player A passes the ball to an inside shoulder running player B. Player A loops player B and retrieves the ball on the far side. Once the ball is passed to player C, the coach calls a number and the player must use evasion skills to run into that space. (In our example, the coach calls 2.) The ball is then placed at the other side of the tubes and all players re-align to attack back up the channel.

To increase difficulty
■ Run with one active defender in place of the middle tackle tube.
■ Run against two defenders active – the coach chooses which tubes to replace.

Fig. 2.57

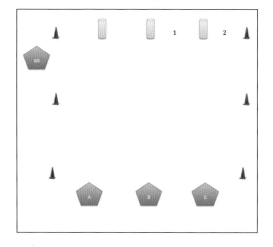

Fig. 2.58

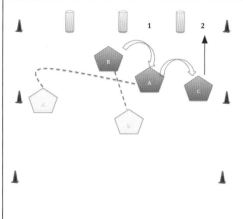

CHAPTER 3 – THE BREAKDOWN

This chapter contains the following drills designed to develop skills in the breakdown.

Ball Placement Practice

Basic Body Height Drill

Basic Ball Placement

Basic Ruck Securer Drill

Grip the Ball Strongly

Pre-Contact Footwork (1)

Pre-Contact Footwork (2)

Spin in Contact (1)

Spin in Contact (2): Body Height

Leg Drive (1)

Leg Drive (2)

Body Height and Decision-Making in Contact (1)

Body Height and Decision-Making in Contact (2)

Contact Decision-Making

Decision-Making at the Ruck (1)

Decision-Making at the Ruck (2)

Leg Drive with Decision-Making

Pick and Drive

Speed up Slow Ball at the Ruck

Changing Body Position Under Pressure

Counter-Rucking

Leg Drive and Back Door Offload Through Contact

Body Height and Targeting a Defender

Forklift

Decision-Making Against the Clock

CHAPTER 3

The Breakdown

To paraphrase a movie quotation: the first rule that you must learn about the break-down is – you don't create breakdowns. The second rule about the breakdown is – you don't create breakdowns!!

In essence, a breakdown should be seen as a failure to breach the gain line which is how you should look at the game of rugby generally – a territorial game that requires movement through a gain line to achieve a score. A breakdown stops that from happening and everything you can do to prevent a break-down from happening should ultimately bring you success in getting over the gain line.

It should also be noted that rugby should be seen as a non-contact game in which, if you do things correctly, there is no need for you to make contact with anyone. However, in reality, contact doesn't just happen, it is sometimes actively encouraged by coaches. There is a belief that by setting up a contact situation, it can allow you to create a pattern where you as the coach can control the posses-sion of the ball. Possession stats usually mean a winning edge but unless you have some thoughts on breaching a gain line to go with that possession, you are onto a loser.

The breakdown is an area that needs to be developed, grown and taught at nearly every session of rugby that you complete. All sessions need to be competitive but based around a learning style with which you and your team are comfortable. In attack, the breakdown is about looking after the ball

and having It available to the scrum half in a way that they can use quickly. In defence, It is about getting your body over the ball, chal-lenging the tackled player/clearers in a way that allows your defence to re-organize.

On the long journeys that I sometimes have to make, I love listening to podcasts; one of these was an interview with manager and talent agent Barry Katz, about the advice he would give to aspiring actors:

> If you want to be successful at an audition, it is fair to say that the director and the producers already have a 'type' in their mind – a person they want to play the role. You are already up against it so you have to go in and change their mind – you have to create a moment in the room.

The same is true of the breakdown. When your players walk on the field, they have to create a moment every time they enter a ruck or they will be unsuccessful. They will think you haven't seen their efforts or even acknowledged their work but you really have.

One of my coaches when I was a youth once said that a ruck was more akin to a basket of washing dropped on the floor than what the coaching books call a ruck. It is intense, energetic, and even a little life-affirming if I am honest; going into a melée and emerging as the person who created the 'moment' is something special indeed.

BALL PLACEMENT PRACTICE

Once a tackle has been made, placing the ball away from the tackler is important but doing so while you are in control of the ball is also important. Try this drill to enhance this small but very important area at the breakdown.

How it works

Fig. 3.1 Player 1 (P1) lies on their side as if they are just about to place the ball back at the ruck. Player 1's feet must touch a line – any one of the lines on a rugby field will suffice. Player 2 (P2) kneels down next to them.

Note: this is a drill that can involve all of your team spread across the lines of the field.

Fig. 3.2 The coach calls one of the following three words: 'waist', 'knees', or 'ankle'. (In our example, 'ankle' was called.) P2 lies on the area stated by the coach and P1 then has to fight to get the ball back to the line as quickly as possible and return to the start position. P2 returns to the kneeling position. P1 can go over or under P2 to touch the line with the ball.

To increase difficulty
■ Add 'chest' to the words where P2 can fall.

Fig. 3.1   *Fig. 3.2*

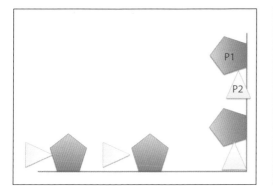   

BASIC BODY HEIGHT DRILL

I am often asked what is the best way to make sure players drive over the ruck in a low body position. As with all skills, players learn better from practical experience and this activity highlights one simple facet for mini players: being low can make things work better. You can then transfer what you have learned in this really fun activity to your ruck practice sessions.

How it works

Fig. 3.3 Organize the players into groups of four to six players. Three players on the 5m line and three on the 15m line with one tackle tube.

Fig. 3.4 Get a player low to drive the tackle tube across to the other side with their shoulder. Once there, a different player will drive the tube back, and so on.

Note: as the players become more fatigued, they will start to raise their body height. This will make the bag harder to push as they are driving the bag into the ground and not across the surface – a good lesson to learn.

Fig. 3.3

Fig. 3.4

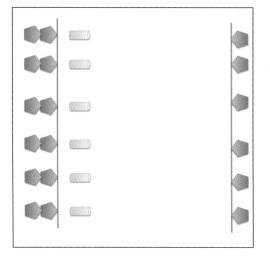
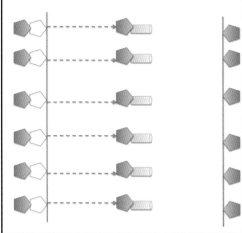

BASIC BALL PLACEMENT

Although it may seem a simple premise, the main hindrance to quick ball is how quickly your scrum half can dig the ball out of a ruck or even at a scrum. These vital split seconds can make all the difference to exploiting a space that your team has created or giving the defence time to reorganize. To show your team how much time can be saved by having good ball placement, try this little drill.

How it works

Fig. 3.5   Place a line of tackle tubes lengthways on the 22m line – six should be enough. At the back, put a player and at one side of the field, put a scrum half.

Fig. 3.6   Start timing the drill. Starting on the touch-line, the scrum half passes to P1.

P1 puts the ball at the back of the tackle tube and touches the tube ensuring P1's chest is over the ball and their legs are back. The scrum half must retrieve the ball and pass it to P2 who repeats what P1 did and so on until the ball gets to P6. Stop timing the drill.

For the second run through, all of the players must now put the ball between their ankles and lean on the tube. When the times are compared, it should highlight how important ball placement (close to the back of the ruck) is to exploiting a defence because the scrum half didn't have to reach into the ruck for the ball.

Fig. 3.5

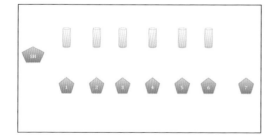

Fig. 3.6

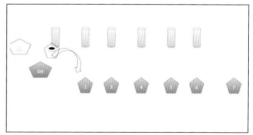

BASIC RUCK SECURER DRILL

Once the opposition have been cleared away from the ball at a ruck, the next player has to secure that area, waiting for his scrum half to pass the ball away and to challenge any defender wishing to start a counter-ruck. Therefore a drill is required to rehearse basic body positioning for the person in this position.

How it works

Fig. 3.7   Lie a tackle tube on the floor with a ball placed behind it. On the far side of the tube are two tackle shields. The nominated player places his hands on the bag with the ball at his ankles.

Fig. 3.8   When the coach calls a number (in our example, the coach called 1), that shield carrier attacks the securer. Depending on the reaction time of that player, they will either have to hold off the shield or attack it to drive it away from your ball.

Note: ensure you coach your players on the correct body position for taking an impact from the front (head to the side, low body position, etc.).

Fig. 3.7

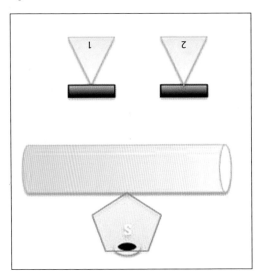

Fig. 3.8

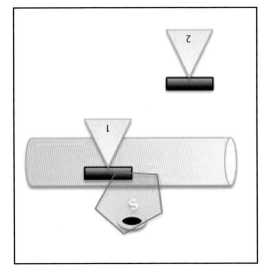

GRIP THE BALL STRONGLY

The very basic part of any contact work is how much control the ball carrier has on the ball once they enter contact. This drill will let you know who has the strongest grip on the ball, with the added bonus of seeing who are the ones in your team that would do anything to possess the ball.

How it works

Fig. 3.9 Two players lie on the floor facing each other. Place a ball in between them so that both players can hold the ball with their arms at full stretch. On the coach's call, both players try to pull the ball into their chest. The winner of the game is the player who has the ball in their possession at the end of ten seconds.

To increase difficulty

Fig. 3.10
■ Each player starts with one hand on the ball and, on the call, brings the other hand from behind their backs to the ball.
■ Add a third player.

Fig. 3.9

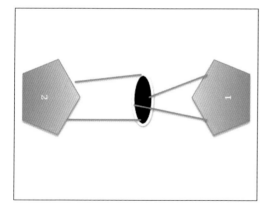

Fig. 3.10

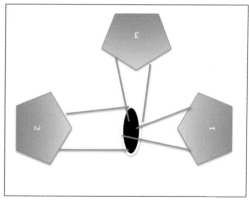

PRE-CONTACT FOOTWORK (1)

There is a belief that the bigger you are, the less footwork you actually need prior to contact. The game is full of players who are simply picked because they can run through people to achieve gain line supremacy. However, unless you are the big kid, footwork is essential to try to get over the gain line.

How it works
Fig. 3.11 Create a channel, 20m × 10m. At 5m intervals, place a different-coloured cone down. Get each player to partner up with someone of the same ability as them. Name one player in team 1 and the other in team 2. Have a ball carrier stand on the first line and their partner stand on the second line.

Fig. 3.12 The ball carrier must get to the end of the channel in ten seconds. The partner tries to stop him. At whatever cone the ball carrier gets stopped at, that's the number of points his team gets. It's a competitive game and making progress down the channel by simply avoiding the tackle scores points.

To increase difficulty
■ Make the channel narrower.
■ Increase the distance between the lines.
■ Have forwards running at back and vice versa (different challenges).

Fig. 3.11

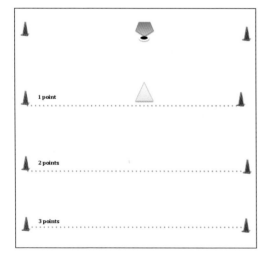

Fig. 3.12

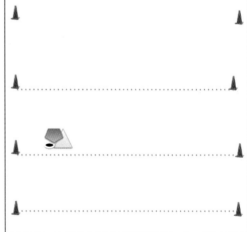

PRE-CONTACT FOOTWORK (2)

How it works

Fig. 3.13   Place a tackle bag to the left or right of a channel parallel with the side. One defender vs. one attacker, of equal ability.

Fig. 3.14   The attacker stands at one end, defender at the other; using the points system from the previous example, the player must pick the ball up and decide to run wide and avoid the tackle but not make progress, or attempt to challenge the defender's agility by trying to make progress closer to the bag.

To increase difficulty
- Place a shield on the floor instead of a tackle tube.
- Make the channel wider.
- Back vs. forward and vice versa.

Fig. 3.13

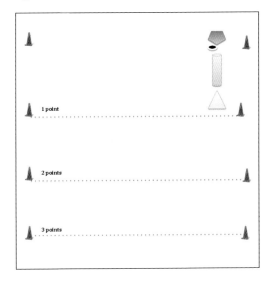

Fig. 3.14

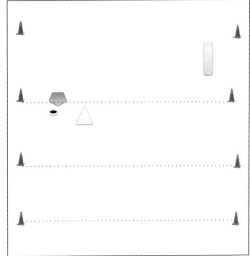

SPIN IN CONTACT (1)

Spinning in contact is generally not seen as much today as it used to be. Although spinning prior to contact does slow you down a little and is less confrontational, there are occasions when spinning can allow you to break free from a defender and move into a space for you to exploit.

How it works
Fig. 3.15 In a 20m × 10m channel, place three tackle tubes about 5m apart in a triangle shape.

Fig. 3.16 Have a player run at the first bag and spin left or right (player's choice to start with). Then spin the opposite way when they approach the second tube (into the gap between the second tubes). This will mean they have to step off both feet in quick succession.

To increase difficulty
- Have the ball change hands in between spins.
- Introduce players to replace the tackle bags – ask them to slap any ball they see to ensure the spin is technically correct.

Note: ensure the ball is carried in two hands and just prior to the spin, the ball stays away from the bag/player throughout the movement. Doing so in this passive environment is good practice before they begin using it in match play.

Fig. 3.15

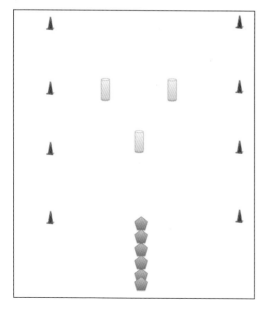

Fig. 3.16

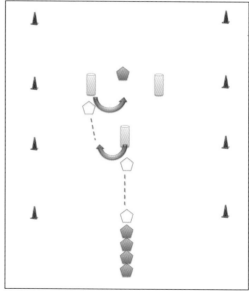

SPIN IN CONTACT (2): BODY HEIGHT

Similar to the previous drill, this one will help your players to take contact on their own terms but with the added ability to stay low, spin out of contact and still be ready to maintain progress down the field in a body position ready to take the next contact.

How it works
Fig. 3.17   In a 20m × 10m channel, place three tackle shields in a line about 5m apart. In front of these shields, place two crossed ski poles. (If your club/school doesn't possess ski poles, use the flagpoles on the side of your playing field.)

Fig. 3.18   A ball carrier runs towards the first set of ski poles that are crossed in front of them. The players go underneath and take sideways contact with the shield. They spin out of contact and repeat the activity down the channel.

To increase difficulty
■ If you stagger the ski poles from left to right, the ball carrier will have to spin, maintain a balance and move across to the next set of ski poles. It will ensure the players understand that lateral movement may be required having spun out of the first contact.

Fig. 3.17

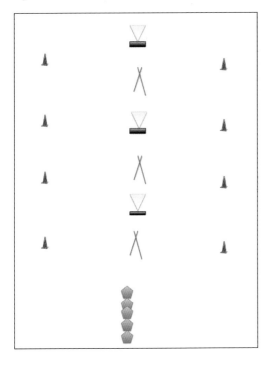

Fig. 3.18

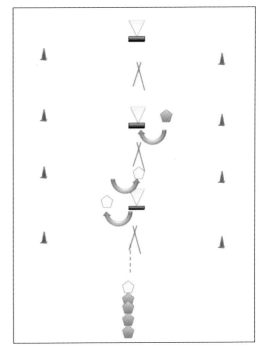

LEG DRIVE (1)

Teams in modern rugby, if they have the resources to do so, have an assessment system for contact play called M.A.C., metres after contact (or Y.A.C., yards after contact). Simply, it is the metres a player has gained once he has met the defender and it will show whether a player has simply run into his defender or moved them to allow some forward momentum into the area behind that defender. This drill will aid in developing this aspect.

How it works

Fig. 3.19 Four defenders spread evenly across a 15m × 20m channel – each holding a tackle shield. In front of the three spaces (named 1, 2 and 3 in this example), place cones to act as 'gates' to the space. 5 metres back, all players wait in a single line for their turn to go.

Fig. 3.20 The player starts their run and the coach immediately calls a number (in this example, 1 is called). The player must hold the ball securely, possess a low body height and break through the two shields who close to make the gap more difficult to get through. Once through the shields, score the try.

Note: ensure your shield-holders leave a small gap for the ball carrier's head to go through. This will ensure the pressure on the ball carrier comes from the side and not directly onto their head.

Fig. 3.19

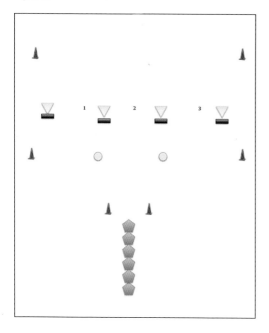

Fig. 3.20

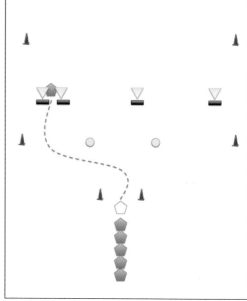

LEG DRIVE (2)

How it works
Fig. 3.21   Set up is similar to the previous drill; however, this time on the try line, directly opposite the start line of the attackers, is a defender.

Fig. 3.22   Once the shields have been reached the coach releases a defender to tackle the ball carrier.

To increase difficulty
- Two defenders and one attacker – judge if the ball carrier can maintain body position effectively in 'heavy' contact.
- Two defenders and two attackers – what does the second attacker do in relation to the actions of the defence (go in, stay out, look for offload, secure possession or drive off the second defender)?
- 3 vs. 3, and you can build the numbers up allowing you to use larger numbers for the session.

Note: to begin with, hold the defender back until after the ball carrier gets through the shields. Once proficient, allow the ball carrier less and less time to make post-contact judgments.

Fig. 3.21

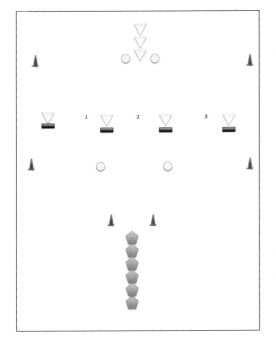

Fig. 3.22

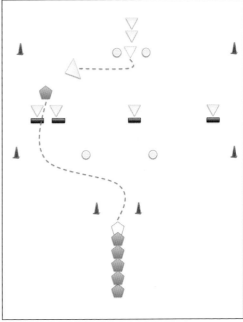

BODY HEIGHT AND DECISION-MAKING IN CONTACT (1)

Sometimes, the ball carrier will be outnumbered and will have to make the decision to take contact on their terms or use evasive tactics to await support. This drill begins that decision-making journey.

How it works
Fig. 3.33 Two defenders against one attacker. Within 10 seconds, can the ball carrier make progress by using their agility skills and low body position to make it to the 3 point line? Note: the defence cannot bring the ball carrier to ground; must be a smother tackle. (This makes the defence work as a team.)

To increase difficulty
■ Two forwards against a back.
■ Make the channel wider to make it harder for the defence.

Fig. 3.33

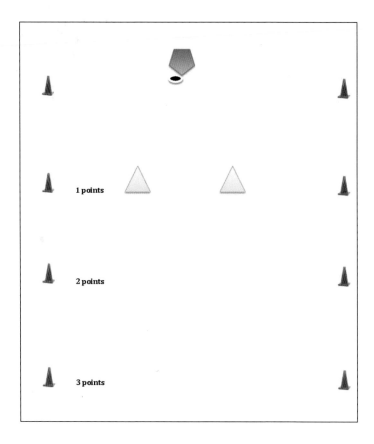

BODY HEIGHT AND DECISION-MAKING IN CONTACT (2)

How it works
Fig. 3.34   Once again, two defenders against one attacker. This time, the defenders are allowed to bring the ball carrier to the ground and steal the ball. Two attackers also wait at the start line.

Fig. 3.35   Once the ball carrier makes contact with the defenders, the two other support players join the game to try to assist the ball carrier to progress the ball up the channel. Activity length: 10 seconds from the point of the ball carrier going to ground.

Fig. 3.34

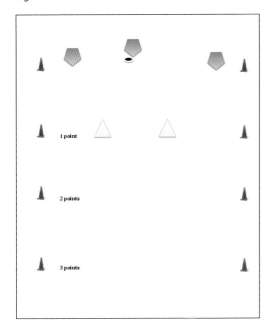

Fig. 3.35

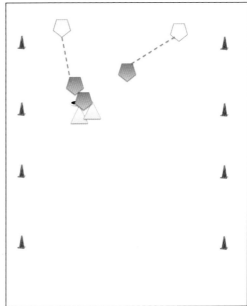

CONTACT DECISION-MAKING

The following activity continues the need for players to continually assess the defence in contact situations.

How it works

Fig. 3.36   Create two channels beside each other, about 15m × 10m each. Have three defenders at the end of each channel, and three attackers in one channel. The coach will call a number between one and three – this is to indicate how many of the defenders are to defend their channel. All three attackers work at all times.

Fig. 3.37   In our example, the coach calls '2' and the attack attempt to score a try.

Fig. 3.38   After 10 seconds or after a try has been scored, the coach makes the attack run back to the start, collect a new ball, and attack in the new channel; the coach calls a new number.

Note: the ball carrier is only allowed to pass after contact has been made with the opposition. They must try and beat the defender 1 vs. 1 first.

To increase difficulty

■ By adding numbers or widening the channels, you can make the drill more or less contact driven depending on needs identified in your team.

Fig. 3.36

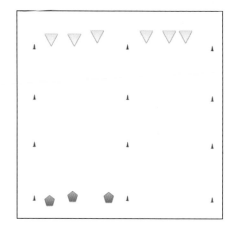

Fig. 3.37

Fig. 3.38

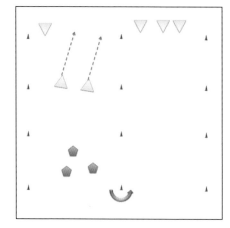

DECISION-MAKING AT THE RUCK (1)

Although you can teach players the technical side of clearing out a ruck with relative ease, it is much harder to give them activities that will clear out immediate dangers as opposed to potential ones. Here is a drill that could help you along this path.

How it works

Fig. 3.39   Two players with shields stand behind a tackle tube laid on the floor – they must be numbered 1 and 2. Two attackers stand 2m behind the tackle bag to the left and right – players marked 'K' are on their knees. Two cones are placed 1m in front of the bag, the same width apart as the tackle bag.

Fig. 3.40   The coach calls 'go' and the two runners behind the tackle bag run around the cone in front of the bag on their side – this signifies a gate! The shield carriers are facing the coach and he holds up one or two fingers to signify which one of the shield carriers steps over the bag. (In our example, the coach holds up one finger.) The bags must be driven back over the tackle tube with the most immediate threat driven back first.

Fig. 3.39

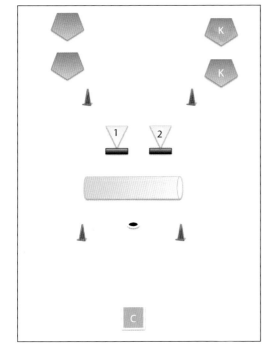

Fig. 3.40

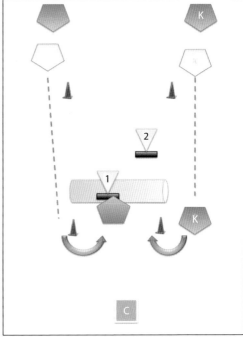

DECISION-MAKING AT THE RUCK (2)

How it works
Fig. 3.41   The set-up for this drill is the same as the previous drill but this time a ball carrier (BC) stands between the cones at the front of the tackle tube.

Fig. 3.42   On the coach's call, the same process begins as before, but now the ball carrier falls in front of the tackle tube to create a more realistic tackle area.

To increase difficulty
■ Allow the shield carriers the choice of whether they come over the bag or not. Will the support runners pick and go or just stay over the ball protecting it? What would you like them to do?

Fig. 3.41

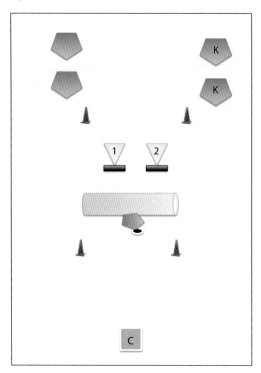

Fig. 3.42

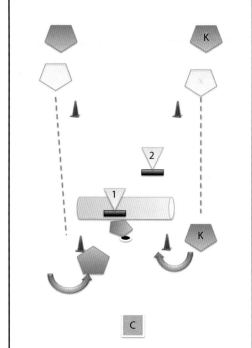

LEG DRIVE WITH DECISION-MAKING

A progression from the previous two drills, this time we introduce extra attackers and defenders into the activity to make it more game-realistic.

How it works

Fig. 3.43 When the drill starts, a ball carrier (BC) and two support players (S1 and S2) are released immediately. The ball carrier runs to the gap called by the coach, the two support players run through the 'gates' not called. The ball carrier breaks through the shields and then must decide whether to use the support runners.

Fig. 3.44 Once the shield has been broken through, two defenders are released.

To increase difficulty
Fig. 3.45
■ Play multiple phases.
■ Attackers must score within a set number of passes.

Fig. 3.43

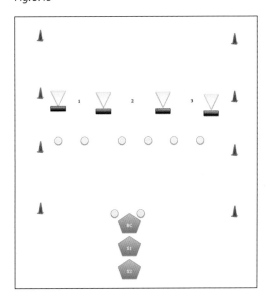

Fig. 3.44

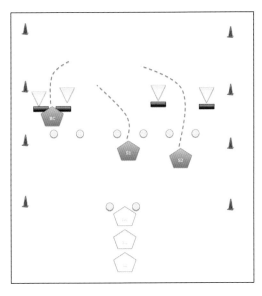

Fig. 3.45

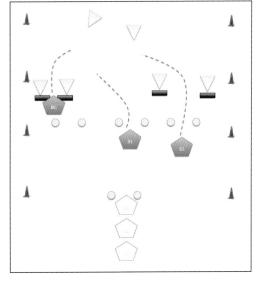

PICK AND DRIVE

The secret to a pick and go is firstly to ensure you carry the ball at a low height and drive into a space created by a person who clears the ground of defenders in front of you in a legal manner. It's a long process to master but this drill will begin the process.

How it works

Fig. 3.46 Create two 5m-wide channels. At various points, place crossed ski poles with a tackle shield behind them.

Fig. 3.47 A ball carrier goes low enough to get under the poles and then drives into the shield. As they fall, a supporting runner clears out the ruck with a third player picking the ball up and moving under ski poles in the other channel. The fourth player supports the player who picked the ball up and went into the new channel.

Fig. 3.46

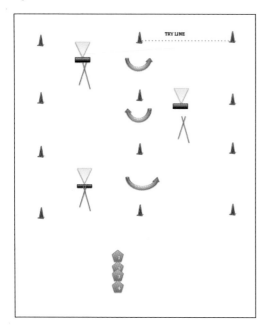

Fig. 3.47

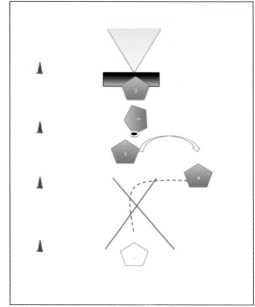

SPEED UP SLOW BALL AT THE RUCK

The problem with slow ball from a ruck is that it allows the defence much more time to get its house in order, making it much harder for you to break through their defensive line. Unless you wish to kick the ball away or make a play that will gain you territorial advantage, you have to disrupt the defence to turn slow ball into quick ball, allowing you the chance to exploit the defence before they have a chance to re-organize. This activity is called 'a wrap' and is one way to turn slow ball into quick.

How it works

Fig. 3.48 Place the ball on the 5m line near touch. Have ten players in attack and five in defence. Have five attackers take the ball into contact and recycle the ball – the coach counts to five to allow the defence to organize. The attack set up a three-man 'pod' – one to catch the ball (C) and two to protect them after they catch the ball.

Fig. 3.48

Fig. 3.49 The scrum half (SH) passes the ball to the catcher in the pod who turns sideways while the protectors go over the top of the catcher.

Fig. 3.50 The SH runs after the ball and the catcher passes the ball immediately back to the SH who runs at the defence, drawing them in and then passes out wide.

Note: the ball receiver in the three-man group must remain very low and in a strong body position while his 'assistants' drive over the top and protect the ball.

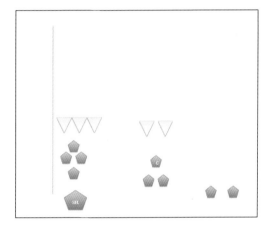

Fig. 3.49

Fig. 3.50

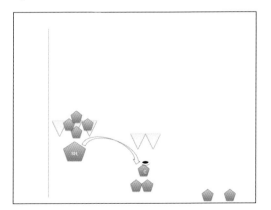

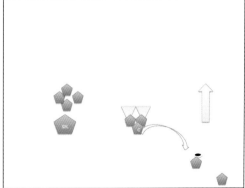

CHANGING BODY POSITION UNDER PRESSURE

When working with midi players (aged 12–17), having them think under pressure is key to their successful transition to adult play. In contact situations, they will hear verbal commands from better-placed colleagues asking them to perform a task while they are under the most demanding of situations. This activity gives such an example and can also be completed as part of a warm-up.

How it works
Fig. 3.51 Two players face each other in a 5m × 5m square. Each side is numbered 1 to 4. One player has a ball; the other places his hands on the ball carrier's shoulders.

Fig. 3.52 On the call of 'go', the ball carrier tries to get to the floor while maintaining possession of the ball. After two seconds of wrestling, the coach calls a number and the ball carrier must push the ball towards that line – they do not have to reach the line (in our example, the coach has called 'two'). The other player stops trying to steal the ball and tries to stop the ball carrier pushing the ball out.

To increase difficulty
■ Two defenders versus a ball carrier.

Fig. 3.51

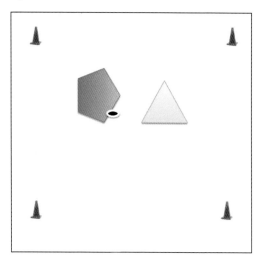

Fig. 3.52

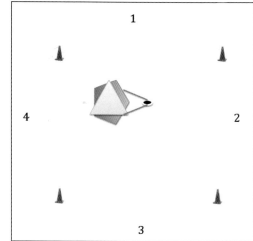

COUNTER-RUCKING

The ability to instigate a counter-ruck at a breakdown the opposition believe to be secure in their favour is a difficult team skill to master. This activity will aid that progress to better team awareness.

How it works

Fig. 3.53   Three players face down a 5m × 10m channel. In the middle of the channel is a tackle tube placed lengthways with a ball.

Fig. 3.54   On the coach's call, the centre player secures the area over the ball in a good body position. He straddles a tackle bag with the ball at his feet, adopting a low body position as if he has just secured the ball. The outside players run around cones at the far end of the channel and drive off the securing player. P1 comes in and gets his hands around an arm/shoulder and lifts up; P2 comes in and using the tackle bag as a guide, drives into the space created by player 1's lift, then drives away the attacking player over his own ball.

To increase difficulty

■   Take the tackle bag away; use a player on the ground with a ball and an attacker to protect the ball.

Fig. 3.53

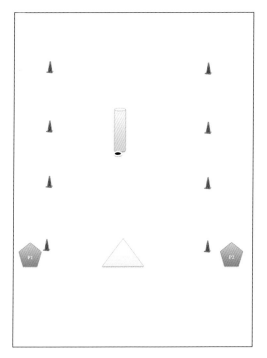

Fig. 3.54

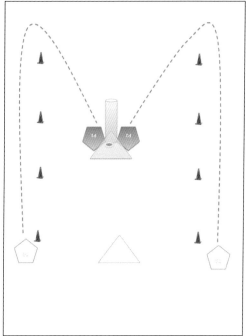

LEG DRIVE AND BACK DOOR OFFLOAD THROUGH CONTACT

On the surface this is a simple enough activity; however, it does involve good dexterity, agility and body height to perform successfully.

How it works
Fig. 3.55   Create three channels – the middle channel is 10m wide, with a 2m channel on either side.

Fig. 3.56   On the coach's call, the ball carrier (BC) runs to the end of the smaller channel while two support players enter the middle channel. The ball carrier sidesteps into the middle channel and attacks the shields. The ball carrier breaks through the shields and 'offloads' the ball with one hand to one of the supporting players once they are through – commonly known as passing out the back. (In our example, the ball was offloaded to player 2.)

To increase difficulty
■   Have a coach or an injured player stand about 5m behind the tackled shields. Once the ball carrier has broken through, have the player point to the left or the right. The ball carrier must pass the ball opposite to the direction shown – this simulates a defender moving that way so the ball must be passed to the free support runner.

Fig. 3.55

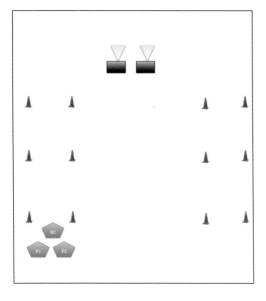

Fig. 3.56

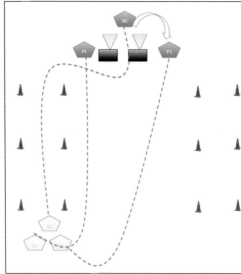

BODY HEIGHT AND TARGETING A DEFENDER

Although your players may arrive at the breakdown thinking they need to drive an opposition player off the ball, on many occasions they will need to change from their first role and transfer their energies into securing the ball from an oncoming defender.

How it works
Fig. 3.57   Work in teams of three – two working, one resting. Each three-man team has a tackle tube and a tackle shield. P1 drives the tackle tube across the floor while in front of the tube; P2, walking backwards, holds a tackle shield.

Fig. 3.58   On coach's call, P2 runs towards P1. P1 raises from driving the tube and changes their body height to drive P2 away from the tube. Rotate the three players so each has a different role after every contact.

Fig. 3.57

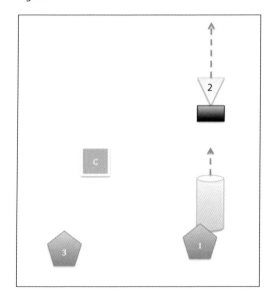

Fig. 3.58

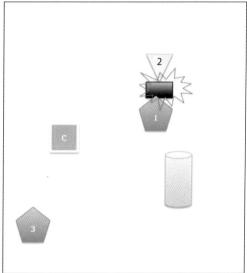

FORKLIFT

This drill is among the hardest drills to do in a contact session as it requires good upper body strength and two or more players being on the same wavelength to make it successful. This drill is designed to combat opposition who roll onto your side of the ball in an effort to slow the ball down. If there is one of your players in a game who can partially lift this player, then this drill will help with the rest.

Fig. 3.59

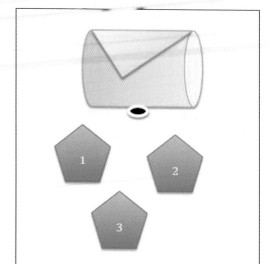

How it works

Fig. 3.59   A defender lies across a tackle tube with a ball they can fall on when the drill begins. Two attackers kneel at arm's length with a third player one arm's length further back.

Fig. 3.60   On coach's call, the player rolls from the tube onto the ball. The two kneeling players try to grab the player and begin to lift back onto the other side of the tube.

Fig. 3.61   The third player uses any power generated to aid the front two players in driving off the defender.

Fig. 3.60

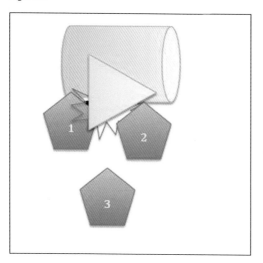

Fig. 3.61

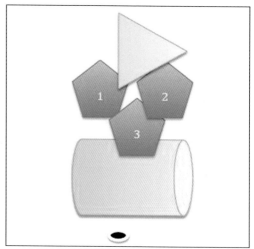

DECISION-MAKING AGAINST THE CLOCK

Players thrive on competition so here's an activity where players in pairs can challenge their team mates using tackle tubes over a set time period. It is high intensity with little risk of injury – and it's great fun.

How it works

Fig. 3.62   Place two tackle tubes in each corner of a 10m × 10m grid. Each corner is numbered and has one player to help 're-set' the corner once the workers have completed the task (marked as 'R' in the example). One tube is standing upright (U) ready to be tackled out of the grid while the other is lying lengthways ready to be driven out.

Fig. 3.63   The coach calls a number and the first arriving player tackles the upright bag (simulates an arriving defender) while the other drives the other bag out of the grid. Once both players return to their feet, the coach calls another number. The winning team is the one that drives the most tubes out of the grid in the set time limit.

Fig. 3.62

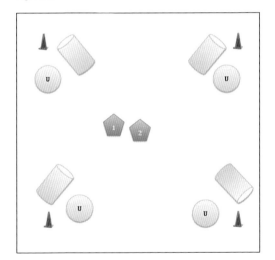

Fig. 3.63

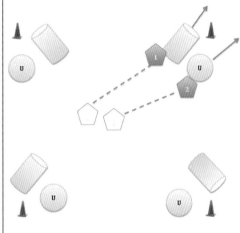

CHAPTER 4 – THE LINE-OUT

This chapter contains the following drills designed to develop skills in the line-out.

First Steps of Lifting in the Line-out

Throwing (1)

Throwing (2)

Off the Top Ball to 9 (1)

Throwing (3)

Jumping Warm-Up (1)

Jumping Warm-Up (Group)

Lifters' Warm-Up

Jumper or Lifter Agility Warm-Up

Pod Movement Drill

Group Lifting Drill

Five-Man Line-out Drill

Off the Top Ball to 9 (2)

CHAPTER 4

The Line-Out

Thanks to the current prevalence of modern video analysis at all levels of the game, the line-out is one of the most keenly contested areas of the modern game. It requires players to have multiple option calls, agility, explosive lifting and jumping skills allied to a ground-in capacity for subterfuge.

If you have a weak line-out presence, oppositions will purposely kick the ball off the field of play to place you under psychological pressure; in contrast, a strong line-out gives you a very powerful attacking tool if you are more proficient than your opponents.

Off the top ball at the back allows you to exploit the farthest reaches of the field while the 20m gap between you and your opponents' back line is ground you can use to devastating effect. Rolling mauls allow you to physically dominate a retreating pack and if released on the front foot, gives your backs front foot ball which they can use to put a runner into a space before the opposition has a chance to adjust.

To become proficient at a line-out takes many, many hours of significant and committed practice and in this chapter, I will give you

a few ideas on how to invigorate a line-out session with fun and challenging activities, whilst also ensuring that the key points you wish to make as a coach are strongly adhered to.

At the top levels of the game there are multiple assets and personnel who can aid the player with developing their skills, but what happens when you are a single coach, with only a few balls, cones, and bags at your disposal? This is a more common situation than many would believe.

With this chapter, in keeping with the theme of this book, I have deliberately designed the activities for the grassroots coach with a limited number of assistant coaches or even balls available to them.

Note: a simple solution would be to give your hooker twenty balls and throw one after the other but most coaches do not have that many available to them until after the session. Which raises a good point – if kicking and line-out throwing is so important to your game, why ask your key players to put in the effort after training? Shouldn't you make it a part of your training session?

FIRST STEPS OF LIFTING IN THE LINE-OUT

Wherever you are in the world, eventually, we all have to teach our forwards to lift in the line-out.

How it works
Fig. 4.1 You require a thrower (T), a jumper (J), two lifters (L) and two assistant lifters (AL). Place the two lifters in the correct position to the front and rear of a line-out jumper.

Once they are in the correct position, the two assistants take hold of the shorts of the jumper to the left and right of the main lifters. What you have created is a four-man lifting team. At first, all four will lift at the same effort level. However, once you as the coach are happy with the technical side of the jump and lift, the assistants can reduce their effort levels. Finally, the assistants remove their hands from the jumper and simply stand as catchers should the lift go wrong.

Fig. 4.1

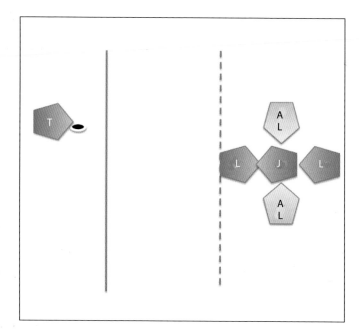

THROWING (1)

Although it is common practice for many throwers to use the goal posts as a target, much of their time is wasted pointlessly retrieving the ball. It is also the case that often a thrower does not have anyone to throw the ball to as the lifters and jumpers are involved in an activity elsewhere. Therefore, try this drill to make limited resources work effectively for you.

How it works
Fig. 4.2   Aiming at the point where the crossbar meets the goal post as a target, a thrower (T) with a ball in hand stands 5m away with two assistants. One assistant (A1) stands directly opposite the thrower on the other side of the posts. The other assistant (A2) stands with a second ball.

Fig. 4.3   Should the ball miss the target, A2 passes the ball to the thrower while A1 retrieves the ball and passes it to A2. Should the ball hit the target, A2 passes the ball to the thrower and retrieves the previously thrown ball.

Fig. 4.2

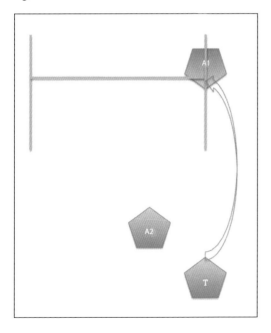

Fig. 4.3

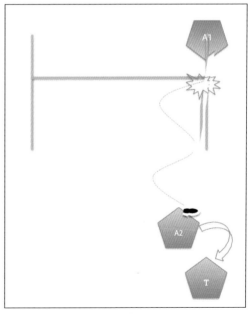

THROWING (2)

With a similar set-up to the previous activity, this exercise allows the thrower to practise throws of differing distances.

How it works
Figs 4.4 and 4.5   Aiming at the point where the crossbar meets the goal post as a target, a thrower (T) with a ball in hand stands 5m away with two assistants. One assistant (A1) stands directly opposite the thrower on the other side of the posts. The other assistant (A2) stands with a second ball. Starting with cones at the 5m line, every 2m place a cone until you reach 17m – this allows the thrower to practise an over-the-top ball.

Fig. 4.4

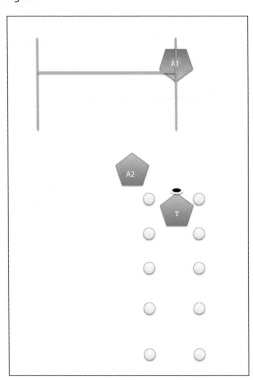

Fig. 4.5

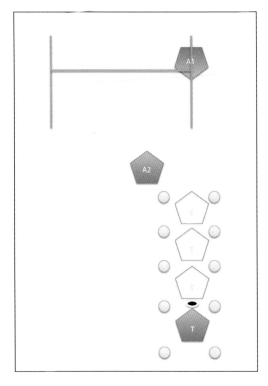

OFF THE TOP BALL TO 9 (1)

This drill can be used as a warm-up or a line-out activity with or without line-out support lifters. It is also perfect for teams where lifting at the line-out is prohibited due to age.

How it works

Fig. 4.6 Using the marking on a field, have a line of jumpers on the 15m line, with throwers on the touch-line and a 9 to act as receiver. Place three marker cones at the 2, 4 and 6 position in a 7-man line-out. (If you only put three into a line-out, just place marker cones down where you would like your players to jump for the ball.)

Fig. 4.7 When the coach calls a number, the jumper runs forward, jumps and catches the ball. On returning to ground, they pass the ball to 9 who returns it to the thrower. (In our example, the coach has called 2.)

To increase difficulty

■ The catcher must catch the ball and turn and pass the ball to the receiver whilst in mid-air (i.e. before they land on the ground).

Fig. 4.6

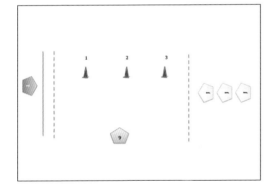

Fig. 4.7

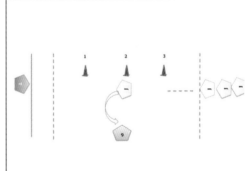

THROWING (3)

How it works

Fig. 4.8 Similar use of assistants to the previous drill throwing, but this time, 2m in front of the thrower is a player holding a tackle shield.

Fig. 4.9 The shield holder tries to block the throw by looking at the body language of the thrower. The thrower's target area remains the same.

Fig. 4.8

Fig. 4.9

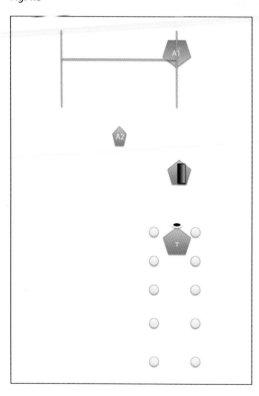

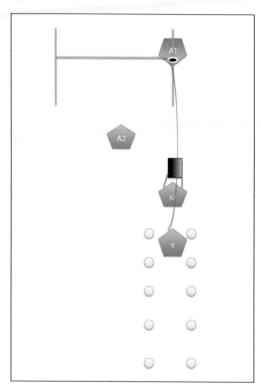

JUMPING WARM-UP (1)

We sometimes forget that completing a generic warm-up at the start of a session isn't enough when specific activities need to be addressed. Here is a drill to help jumpers get prepared for their part of the lifting process.

How it works
Fig. 4.10   Have one jumper stand on the touch-line and the other on the 5m line with a ball.

Fig. 4.11   The jumper throws the ball over the head of J1 and they jump up, catch the ball and pull the ball back sharply to their chest, mimicking what they do in a match. J1 then throws over the head of J2 and the drill continues.

Fig. 4.10

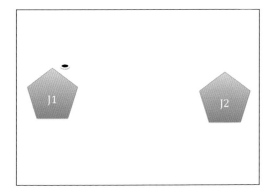

Fig. 4.11

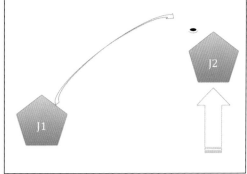

JUMPING WARM-UP (GROUP)

How it works

Fig. 4.12   Have one line of jumpers stand on the touch-line and the other line on the 5m line with a ball. The jumper throws the ball over the head of the opposite player.

Fig. 4.13   The receiver jumps up to catch the ball but they must put the ball back over the head of their opposite player before they touch the ground (catch and pass over their head whilst in the air).

To increase difficulty

Fig. 4.14

- Increase the distance between the two jumpers.
- Once they have caught and passed the ball, run to the back of the opposite line.

Fig. 4.12

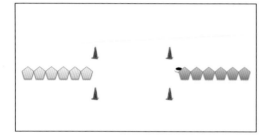

Fig. 4.13

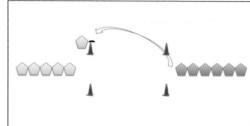

Fig. 4.14

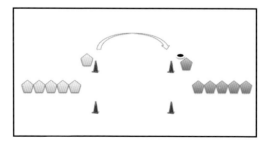

LIFTERS' WARM-UP

Previously we have warmed up the thrower and the jumper but now we need to look at warming up the lifters.

How it works
Fig. 4.15 Working in pairs, place two players 5m away from a tackle tube.

Fig. 4.16 When they are ready, both players run in, place the palms on their hands on the tube, squeeze and then lift/push the tube up in the air. Lower the bag down to the floor, jog back to their starting position and begin again. Ensure correct lifting technique, even at this very early stage.

To increase difficulty
- Once the players have the tube in the air, ask them to turn 180 degrees, lower the tube and jog backwards to their partner's start line.

Fig. 4.15

Fig. 4.16

JUMPER OR LIFTER AGILITY WARM-UP

In the modern line-out, effective and speedy movement is essential in allowing you to move the ball to a part of the line-out.

How it works
Fig. 4.17   Create a diamond with three different-coloured cones in the middle. One player stands inside the diamond. Each corner of the diamond is given a number.

Fig. 4.18   To start the drill, the coach calls a number. The player runs around the cone but as the player runs back into the diamond, the coach calls two colours which the player must touch and then sprint out of the diamond in any direction. In our example, the coach called cone 4 then 'red' and 'green'.

Fig. 4.17

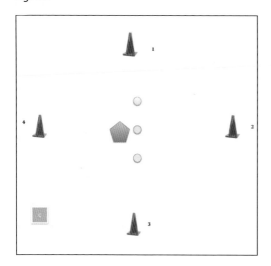

Fig. 4.18

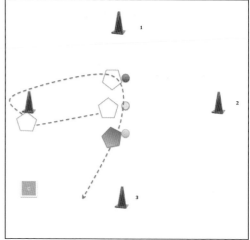

POD MOVEMENT DRILL

An effective line-out consists of a good throw and the jumpers and lifter all working in harmony. This drill begins the process of throwing, movement and effective lift to meet a ball in the air.

How it works
Fig. 4.19   Create a diamond with three different-coloured cones in the middle. Two jumpers and a lifter stand inside the diamond near the cones. Each corner of the diamond is given a number.

Fig. 4.20   On coach's call, L1 runs around cone 1, L2 runs around cone 3, and J runs around cone 3. All return to the middle.

Fig. 4.21   The coach then calls a colour, which the jumper needs to get to and be lifted. (In our example, 'red' was called.)

To increase difficulty
- Have a thrower put a ball in the air ready for the lifter to retrieve.

Fig. 4.19

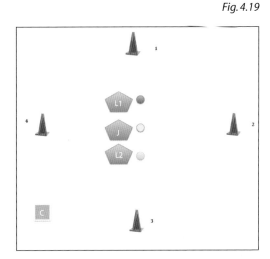

Fig. 4.20

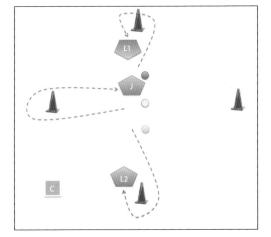

Fig. 4.21

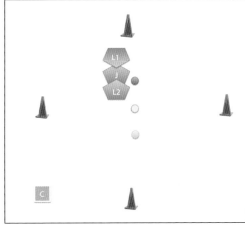

GROUP LIFTING DRILL

When you have a number of lifters and jumpers to work with, boredom on wet, cold winter evenings can make even the best players inattentive. This is a simple activity that allows everyone to stay involved while allowing you to look at the technical aspects of your players' line-out roles.

How it works

Fig. 4.22   Place three coloured cones between the 5m and the 15m line. Place all of your throwers (T) on the touch-line. Place all of your lifters (L) 10m to the right and the Jumpers (J) 10m to the left.

Fig. 4.23   When the coach calls a colour, the jumper runs to that cone and sets for the jump. The lifters get into position and when the jumper starts their movement, the thrower puts the ball in. In mid-air, the ball is thrown back to the thrower and a new set of players gets ready. (In our example, the coach called 'red'.)

To increase difficulty

- Give the pod a time limit to get into the line and retrieve the ball.
- Put a pod against them to see who gets up first – thrower throws to the first one up in the air.

Fig. 4.22

Fig. 4.23

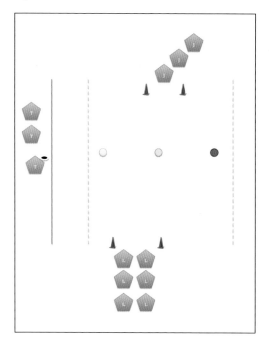

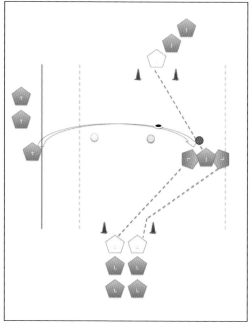

FIVE-MAN LINE-OUT DRILL

In modern rugby, it is only the props who don't lift and jump. This drill helps keep all back five players alert to the possibility of an ever-changing role while making your line-out as effective as possible.

How it works

Fig. 4.24 Set up a line-out where props are placed at numbers 1 and 5, evenly spread out. Have a thrower (T) and a person acting as a receiver (R).

Fig. 4.25 When the coach calls a number that player is the jumper and the players alongside are the lifters. Due to the specialized nature of the roles, the coach will only call 2, 3 or 4. In our example, the coach has called 4.

Fig. 4.24

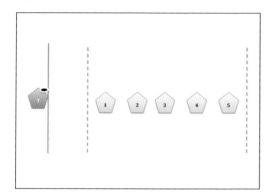

Fig. 4.25

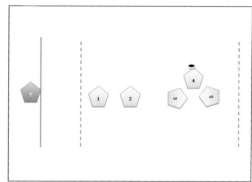

OFF THE TOP BALL TO 9 (2)

A progression from the previous drill but this time you can bring in lifters.

How it works
Fig. 4.26   Very similar set up to the previous drill, but this time, on the opposite side of the line-out to the 9, there is a line of lifters.

Fig. 4.27   Coach still calls a number but this time the jumper and the lifters must work together to get maximum height, with speed to retrieve the ball. Once in possession at the top of the jump, ball must be passed safely and quickly to 9 who passes back to the thrower.

To increase difficulty
■ Place a line of lifter and jumpers behind the 9, who run and defend against the jump. The call is made secretly to the attacking team and the defenders must react against it.

Fig. 4.26

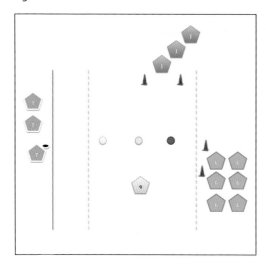

Fig. 4.27

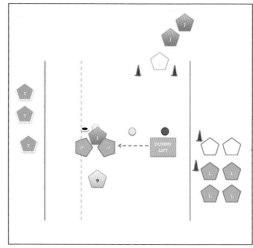

CHAPTER 5 – SCRUM CONFIDENCE

This chapter contains the following drills designed to develop confidence in the scrum.

Scrum Confidence

Muscle Memory

Body Position Test (1)

Body Position Test (2)

Hooker Strike (1)

Hooker Strike (2)

8 and 9 at the Scrum

Back Row T-Drill

Scrum Fatigue (1)

Scrum Fatigue (2)

CHAPTER 5

Scrum Confidence

The *bête noire* of the modern game is the scrum. It is a much maligned unit skill that has been the source of many people calling for its re-imagining as soon as possible. Every few years, there is an adjustment to the sequence or the laws surrounding the scrum that for a short time solve an issue, just prior to another one emerging.

Teams spend many, many hours per season building an effective scrum only to see it fall apart on match day through collapses and recriminations. That is true isn't it? Well – not really. For the majority of players who play the game, the scrum is a contest of wills and techniques as it always has been. Number 8s still get an opportunity to work a move with their back row colleagues, props still have energetic contests with their opposite numbers and for most, the scrum is in rude health. So what's the problem?

Most people admit that the real issues in scrummaging are in the professional game and, whatever your thoughts are on that, most of us deal with the reality of teaching the scrum at the lower ends of the game and at youth level. Coaching the scrum is a slow and methodical process and needs time to ensure that the safety of all is paramount in your thoughts. That doesn't mean that we need to simply stand by a scrum machine for the entire evening while many of the team get cold or bored, or worse.

These drills are about using the time you have available to you in innovative ways that hopefully will spark your imagination for the future. Many of the skills in the scrum can be practised in isolation, which allows you to send off two or three players to work as a group while you continue with the rest of your team's session.

SCRUM CONFIDENCE

When you first start teaching the scrum, the biggest hurdle to overcome is the fear of it collapsing. Try this activity to help build the confidence of your young players.

How it works

Fig. 5.1 In a 1 vs. 1, 2 vs. 2 or 3 vs. 3 scrum, have them stand on either side of a tackle tube. On the 'set' call, they do so over the tackle tube which, because of its height, allows the player to use the bag to maintain their balance should they lose their grip on their opponent's shirt.

Note: as the players become more proficient, you can change the tackle tube for stacked shields which can be taken away one at a time once the players become more competent.

Fig. 5.1

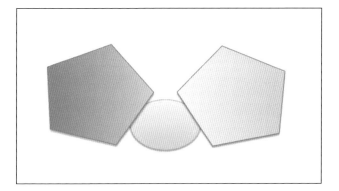

MUSCLE MEMORY

This activity is designed to help build competitive scrums whilst continually being mindful of the players' safety. Using the players' awareness of how their muscles feel when in the correct body positioning for scrummaging, you can allow them to develop their scrummaging in safety.

How it works

Fig. 5.2   Create a 10m × 10m square, each side lined with different-coloured cones. Two forwards work against each other. Allow the players to push against each other.

After 5 seconds, shout 'reset'. The players stop pushing, reset themselves into optimum pushing position and await the next 'go' call.

Note: after each 'reset' call, ask each player to recall their muscles' stresses when they are in the correct body position, realizing that this may not be a possibility for many. This activity would be a great opportunity for a local referee to come and watch and decide the competitive game at the end.

To increase difficulty
■   Create a 3 vs. 3 competition.

Fig. 5.2

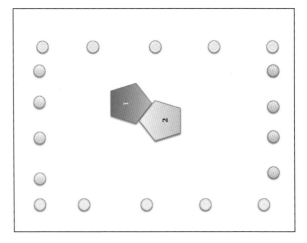

BODY POSITION TEST (1)

This a great drill to see how a player's body positioning holds up under pressure and fatigue.

How it works
Fig. 5.3   Line up four sets of players, in pairs, on the 5m line. All other players stand at the start.

Fig. 5.4   The player runs to pair 1 and drives them back to the try line. Then they return to the 5m line and drive pair 2 back to the try line and so on until the task is complete, and then return to the start.

To increase difficulty
- The coach can increase or decrease the efforts of the pairs being driven – be more aggressive or more passive depending on the effort desired.

Fig. 5.3

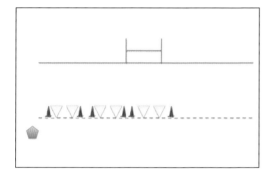

Fig. 5.4

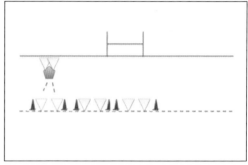

BODY POSITION TEST (2)

How it works
Fig. 5.5   Work in groups of three on the 22m line. Place cones at approximately 5m intervals between the pairs and the try line.

Fig. 5.6   The worker (W) drives the pair back to the first cone and stops. The worker then resets to optimum body position and drives again. They continue on until they reach the try line – then swap around.

To increase difficulty
■ The coach can increase or decrease the efforts of the pairs being driven – be more aggressive or more passive depending on the effort desired.
■ Coach can ask all players to restart on a specific call so everyone drives at the same time.

Fig. 5.5

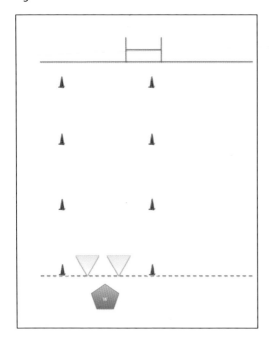

Fig. 5.6

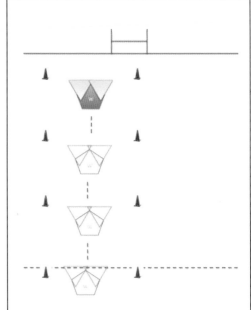

HOOKER STRIKE (1)

The effectiveness of the hooker's strike of the ball in the scrum is the key first part of whether a back row move can be initiated from any set piece (passage of the ball, scrum's position being others). This continuous drill helps the hooker get their technique in order before entering a live scrum.

How it works
Fig. 5.7   The hooker (H) scrummages against the goal post in the same body position as they might be expected to at a live scrum. A feeder (F) puts the ball into the space and the hooker strikes the ball back to the receiver (R) who in turn passes the ball back to the feeder.

To increase difficulty
■   Ask the hooker to lower their body height against the post.

Fig. 5.7

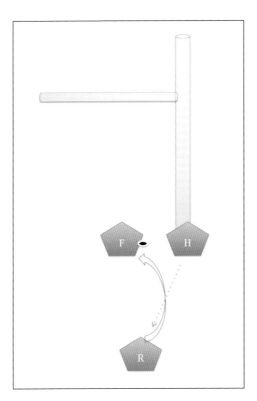

HOOKER STRIKE (2)

This is a follow-on drill making the hooker strike the ball at a target and not just simply pushing the ball back in any direction. This can be a skill required as players work at a higher level of the game or become much more experienced.

How it works
Fig. 5.8   The hooker (H) scrummages against the goal post in the same body position as they might be expected to at a live scrum. A feeder (F) puts the ball into the space and the hooker strikes the ball back to a target (T) called by the receiver (R) prior to the ball being fed to the hooker.

To increase difficulty
■ Ask the hooker to lower their body height against the post.
■ Transfer the drill to a scrum machine and have a full front row participate.

Fig. 5.8

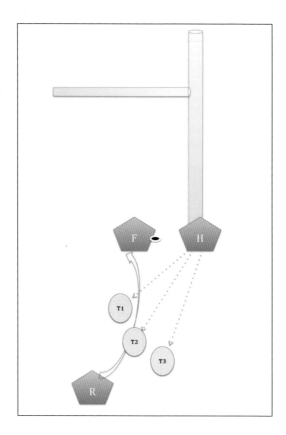

8 and 9 AT THE SCRUM

The number 8 is part of what is called the 'spine' of the team (2, 8, 9, 10 and 15) and whether the ball is moved from a scrum effectively usually starts and finishes with the 8 and the 9 working together. Here is a drill to aid that relationship.

How it works
Fig. 5.9   Working in a 15m × 10m grid, a tackle tube is placed on the left hand side of the grid. D1 places their palms onto the tube. D2 places one hand on the back on D1 and has a ball. 8 stands at the other end of the tube with their palms on the tube. 9 stands behind 8.

Fig. 5.10   D2 passes the ball to 8, who immediately places it on the ground between his legs for the 9. 9 has two choices: pick the ball and try to score, or tap 8 on the shorts for them to pick, and work as a pair to score the try.

Fig. 5.9

Fig. 5.10

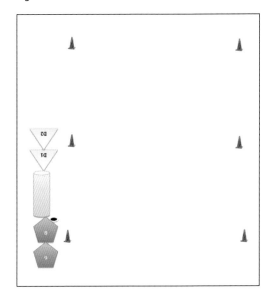

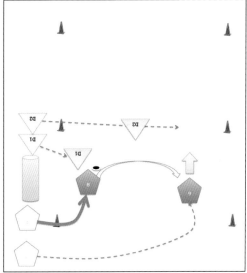

BACK ROW T-DRILL

While the front five are being coached, the back row need to be sent with the back line to acclimatize themselves with what their colleagues are doing and how they can aid the retention of the ball should a score or line break not occur. However, on the rare occasions when the back line do not require them, try this drill just to keep them busy.

How it works
Fig. 5.11 On the right hand side of the field, two tackle tubes are set up in a T-shape. The flankers place their inside hands on the top tackle tube while the 8 places their hands on the back of the second tube. A ball is at the 8's feet with a 9 standing behind them. About 10m away from the T-shape are two tackle shields as targets.

Fig. 5.12 On the coach's call, 8 picks the ball up and falls onto the two tackle shields, presenting the ball as if it were a ruck. The 7 clears out over the top and the 9 retrieves the ball. The 6 decides whether to go outside or inside this ruck to take a pop ball from the 9.

Fig. 5.11

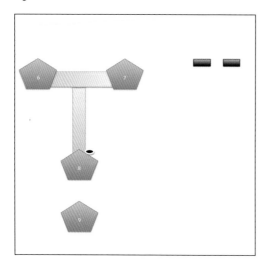

Fig. 5.12

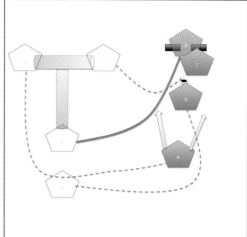

SCRUM FATIGUE (1)

If numbers prevent you from having two full sets of players for a competitive scrum, try this drill to see how your players work under the pressures of fatigue.

How it works
Fig. 5.13   Place a scrum machine (SM) on the try line facing down the field.

Fig. 5.14   Drive the machine to the 22m line – coach shouts 'break' and the players jog to the try line and back to the machine. They reset and drive the machine from the 22m to the half-way line – 'break' – run to the try line and back to the machine. Drive from the half-way line to the far 22m – 'break' – return to their own try line and back to the machine for the final drive from the far 22m to the finish line.

To increase difficulty
■ Place a time limit on reaching the finish line.
■ Drive to every line on the field not just the unbroken ones.

Fig. 5.13

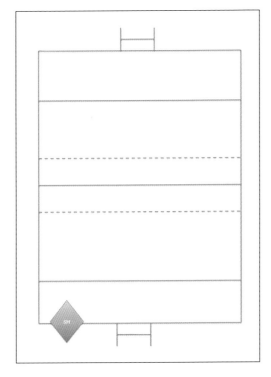

Fig. 5.14

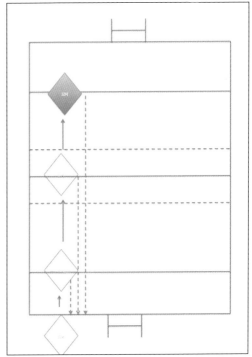

SCRUM FATIGUE (2)

At all times, coaches must try to ensure their players are conditioned enough to work under game-like conditions, which means working at a scrum when fatigued. Try this drill to see where your team currently stands in regards to maintaining their technical skills at the scrum when tired.

How it works

Fig. 5.15 Using the entire rugby field, place several 10m x 10m grids using different-coloured cones. A tackle shield must be available between two players on opposing sides – e.g. opposing tight head props must have a shield between them; opposing hookers must have a shield between them.

Fig. 5.16 Coach calls a colour (red) and a competitive scrum (S) must be set up in that grid. Once completed, Team A must place the shields on the floor and push them to the next grid (green) where the next scrum is to occur. Once completed, the shields are given to Team B and they must push them to the next grid. They continue alternating and scrummaging until the time limit the coach has set for the drill is reached.

To increase difficulty

- Make the losing scrum in each grid push the shields along the floor.
- Increase the distance of 'shield-pushing' between one scrum and the next.

Fig. 5.15

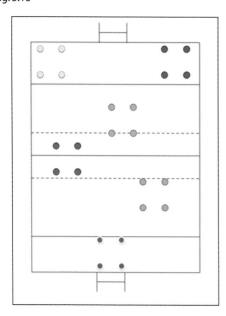

Fig. 5.16

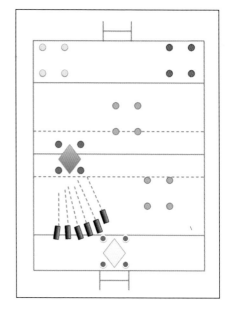

CHAPTER 6 – KICKING

This chapter contains the following drills designed to develop skills in kicking.

Box Kick Height Practice

Box Kick Target Practice

Cross Kick Activity

The Cross Kick: in Goal

Grubber Kick

Chasing a High Ball

Chip Kick Accuracy

Punt Kick Accuracy

Pressurized Drop Goals Game

Continuous Catching/Kicking Drill

CHAPTER 6

Kicking

Everyone fancies themselves as a kicker and as every coach will tell you, the best kickers in your teams are props and flankers – that is, of course, if you base your thinking on what you see at the start of training! Kicking is a highly specialized skill and its introduction into the game at youth level can bring many headaches. As the player progresses to adult rugby, kicking becomes much more of a tactical weapon that needs close supervision and constant review. Below are a few thoughts on kicking.

WHEN TO KICK?

When your team kicks the ball, they are giving the ball away to their opposition. Now this is not as terminal an issue if you have planned for your team to kick. If you want your team to kick in certain parts of the field, that's okay but as a general rule, kicking should only be done if:

■ You get it back – chips and grubber kicks.
■ You can gain ground – to put the line-out as close to the opposition line as possible.
■ To put pressure on the defence – kick into a space where no player from the opposition currently stands.

WHERE TO KICK?

A very famous rugby league coach once said that if you are going to kick, kick to the seagulls. What he meant by that was in matches that are played by the sea, birds land looking for worms in the broken ground so if there are birds there, that's where the space is. If you kick the ball long down the field, then making it bounce as many times as possible means that no opposition player has touched it while you are chasing. So when they do get to the ball, they are under maximum pressure.

WHO KICKS AND WHO CHASES?

Although it might seem a little simplistic, I have always found the best player to kick the ball is the best kicker – you need to find out who that is. Although they might not be the 10, you can adjust your alignment to make sure that player kicks from, say, set pieces.

As for who chases, there are several ideas about this but the most common is for two of the closest players to the estimated landing point to chase the ball. So from a scrum, if the 10 kicks the ball down the field, 12 and 13 chase. If the ball is kicked across the field towards a touchline (wiper kick), 13 and the winger on that side chase. The kicker doesn't chase as by the time they kick and start running, everyone will be too far ahead of them – the kicker stays where they are and covers any clearing/returning kick from the opposition.

Every team has their own strategy for kicking and you need to think about what you want your players to do once the decision to kick has been made.

BOX KICK HEIGHT PRACTICE

A simple activity to try and challenge your 9's ability to get more height on box kicks.

How it works
Fig. 6.1   Place a ball at the base of a goal post with a 9 ready to kick.

Fig. 6.2   The player picks the ball and steps away from the post and tries to clear the top of the post with the kick.

Note: this is a height exercise, not a distance one.

To increase difficulty
■ Two metres back from the goal post, place a defender who tries to charge down the kick as soon as the 9 pulls the ball away from the post.

Fig. 6.1

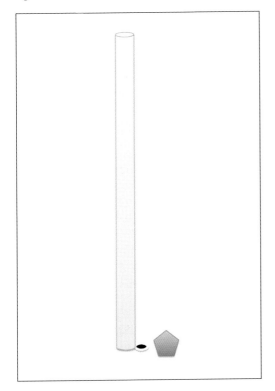

Fig. 6.2

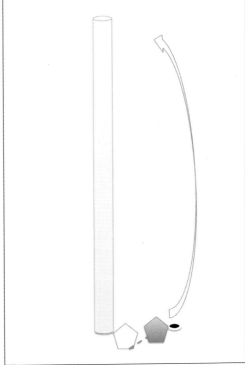

BOX KICK TARGET PRACTICE

Box kicks have become a very potent attacking weapon with accuracy and timing a key component in their success. Here is a practice for your 9 and the chasers to get the accuracy required for a successful box kick.

How it works

Fig. 6.3   Place a tackle shield 1m in front of the 22m line. Use the shield as a target as any player from the opposition could not call a 'mark' outside the 22m. In line with the tackle shield, position a 9 with a ball on the 10m line and a runner to chase the kick. Stand three tackle tubes in front of the ball in a triangle shape. Place a defender behind the tubes to try and block the box kick – they must have a hand on the front tackle tube before the call.

Fig. 6.4   On coach's call, the 9 box kicks the ball to land on the tackle shield, the defender tries to block the kick and the runner chases the ball to catch in mid-air.

To increase difficulty

■ Take the ball back to the half-way line – this means a kick with less height so will be easier to block by the defender.

Fig. 6.3

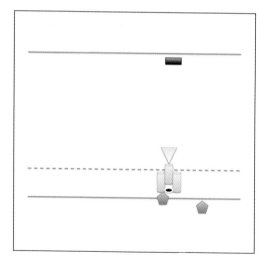

Fig. 6.4

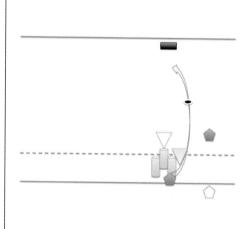

CROSS KICK ACTIVITY

The following activity will help your players get a feel for what it is like to chase a cross-field kick in a fun and competitive way.

How it works

Fig. 6.5 In a wide grid – 30m × 40m – place equal numbers of players on each cone. 5m in front of each cone, place another cone.

Fig. 6.6 A player from line A jogs to the cone 5m in front and cross kicks to a running player from line B. When the line B player catches the ball, he passes the ball to line D. The new player from line D cross kicks the ball to a player running from line C. When the player from line C catches the ball, they pass to line A. Remember: lines A and B work together; lines C and D work together.

Note: the reason you would have a cone in front is to make the players realize that they must run forward before making the kick. To simply face where the kick is to go immediately shows your hand to the opposition in a competitive match. Ask the kickers to run to the cone first and then turn to make the kick.

Fig. 6.5

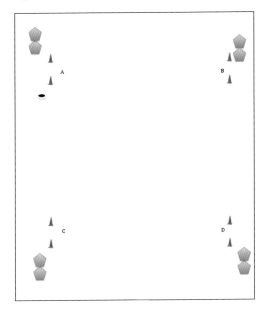

Fig. 6.6

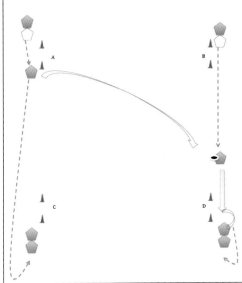

THE CROSS KICK: IN GOAL

Every person who knows about rugby will always tell you that there is space out wide. On television, its usually a co-commentator who can see what we can't who shouts 'numbers' to identify that one team has an overlap on the outside. Passing is one way to get the ball out there but cross kicking is a skill that can get the ball out wide quicker and is devastating if it is practised and planned for.

How it works

Fig. 6.7 A scrum half (SH) stands 10m back from the goal post with a ball. A kicker (K) stands where they would normally stand from phase play in attack. One player acts as the chaser (C) and is placed in the 5m channel. Another player is designated a support runner (S). Place four cones in the corner of the in-goal area as a target for your kicker.

Fig. 6.8 Scrum half passes to kicker. Catcher runs to catch the cross kick which should land near or in-goal or the chaser can tap the ball back to his support runner. The aim of the activity is to score a try.

To increase difficulty
■ Place two defenders in the in-goal area. Let the catcher catch the ball, then the defenders can tackle or try to steal the ball.

Fig. 6.7

Fig. 6.8

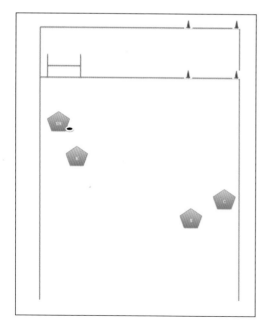
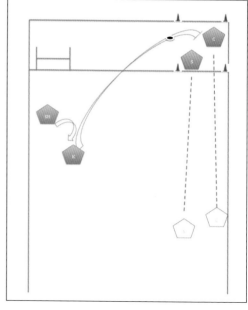

GRUBBER KICK

The grubber kick can be a very effective means of breaching a gain line if a defence comes on a blitz and the opposition do not have a player sweeping behind their frontline defence. As opportunities to grubber kick happen quickly, here is an activity that can replicate that urgency.

How it works
Fig. 6.9 Place a kicker (K) behind a gate. Have a scrum half (SH) stand 10m away, whose role it is to feed the ball to the kicker. 15m in front of the kicker are four numbered gates.

Fig. 6.10 On coach's call, the kicker runs out of the gate to be fed the ball by 9. As soon as the kicker touches the ball, the coach calls a number and the kicker must grubber the ball through that gate. Once completed, the kicker returns to the start and begins again.

To increase difficulty
- Increase the distance from the kicker.
- Decrease the width of the numbered gates.

Fig. 6.9

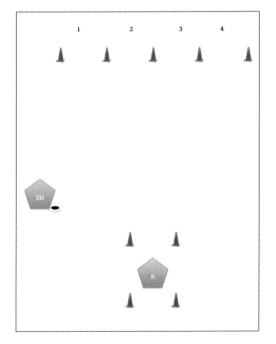

Fig. 6.10

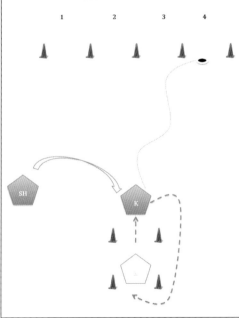

CHASING A HIGH BALL

Kicking with an effective chase to retrieve it behind the opposition's defensive line is still a key attacking weapon if used well. This drill will aid the chasing of a kick by a chasing runner.

How it works
Fig. 6.11   Two teams of three stand 40m apart – closer or further away depending on the ability of your players.

Fig. 6.12   A kicker from one team kicks a high ball for the opposing team to catch. While the kicker is chasing, they look at the person who is setting themselves up to catch the ball   that is your chase target area. When the chaser gets within 10m, the catcher steps away, leaving the chaser to catch the ball without hindrance. The ball is given to a player from the opposing team who kicks and chases the ball back to the other team.

To increase difficulty
Fig. 6.13
■ Have one player from the receiving team hold a tackle shield to hit the catcher once they have the ball in hand.

Fig. 6.11

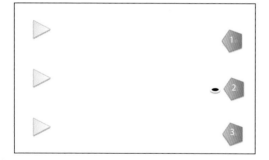

Fig. 6.12

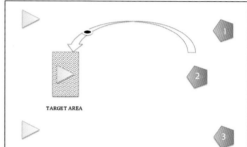

Fig. 6.13

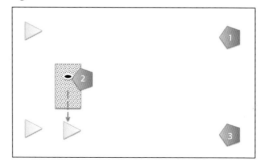

CHIP KICK ACCURACY

When you see a space that you want to chip the ball into, it only takes a small, misplaced drop on the boot to put the ball where it will be of advantage to your opponent. This simple drill will put pressure on your chip kick in a fun and enjoyable way.

How it works

Fig. 6.14   Create a grid roughly 15m × 15m with kickers on each corner (minimum of five). On each side, place a tackle tube as shown.

Fig. 6.15   Player A chips the ball over the tackle tube, runs around the tube to catch the ball, then passes the ball to player B. Player B does the same and gives the ball to player C.

Note: the tackle tube simulates a player you have to run around in a match to retrieve the ball.

Fig. 6.14

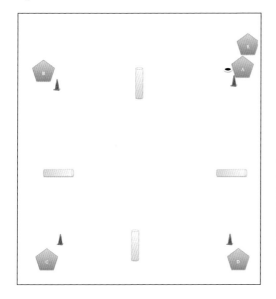

Fig. 6.15

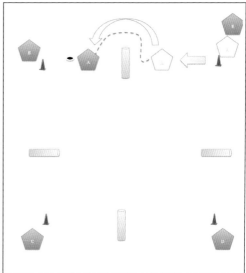

PUNT KICK ACCURACY

The punt kick or the kick from the hands can be completed in two ways: onto the end of the ball or the spiral. Whichever is your team's preferred kicking style, this activity will challenge your players' accuracy.

How it works
Fig. 6.16   Create an arc of six cones around the posts. The distance and angle of the cones away from the posts is dependent on the strength of the kickers in your team. Place a ball at each cone. In one minute, your kicker must punt kick all six balls between the posts. They are allowed to begin at whichever cone they wish. The most difficult kicks will be the ones where the angle to aim at is narrower.

To increase difficulty
■ Increase the distance between the balls and the posts.
■ Change the punt kicks to drop kicks.

Fig. 6.16

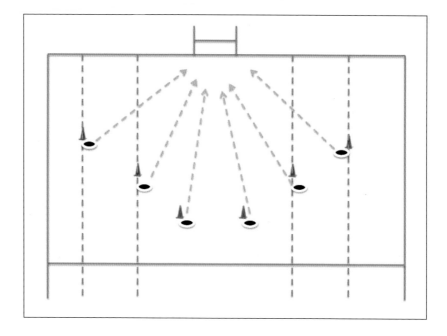

PRESSURIZED DROP GOALS GAME

Everyone in your team thinks they can drop kick. If you leave a few balls lying around before training, it is instinct for all players to have drop kicks and place kicks at goals. Of course, the real test of kickers' mettle is what can they do under pressure. Here is a drill that will help recreate those high-pressure moments.

How it works
Fig. 6.17 Start a contact game with two teams of equal number inside the 22m. If you have the numbers, place a 9–10 combination on both sides.

Fig. 6.18 At various points in proceedings, the coach starts to count down loudly from ten. Before the time runs out, the designated kicker (K) must get into a position or create an opportunity to take a drop at goal, or go for the try.

To increase difficulty
■ Take away the countdown from ten but the kicker must go for the drop kick at some point over the next three phases of play. This allows the kicker to decide when to complete the kick and also keeps the defence from knowing when the drop kick is coming.

Fig. 6.17

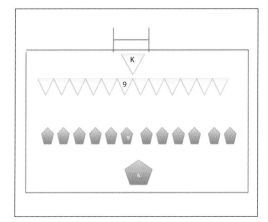

Fig. 6.18

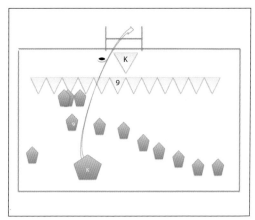

CONTINUOUS CATCHING/KICKING DRILL

When a ball is kicked along the wings (down the tram lines), the ball is often played in field for either a counter-attack or a return kick down field. This drill will allow your wingers and full backs a chance to work repeatedly on their accuracy and techniques in a game-related manner.

Fig. 6.19

How it works
Fig. 6.19   Place a winger on the 5m/22m cross line at either end of the field. Place a full back on the 15m line inside the 22m area. (Or further in-field depending on your winger's passing ability.)

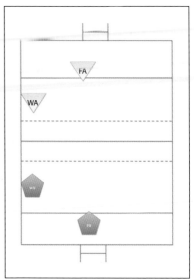

Fig. 6.20   Full back A (FA) kicks the ball down the field to winger B (WB). Winger B catches, passes the ball in-field to full back B (FB) who kicks the ball to winger A (WA).

Note: don't forget to use both sides of the field to ensure challenging both full backs equally.

To increase difficulty
Fig. 6.21
■ If there is space, place the wingers off the field. This will allow practice for possible counter-attack.

Fig. 6.20

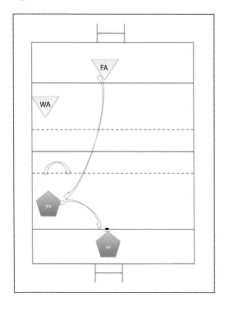

Fig. 6.21

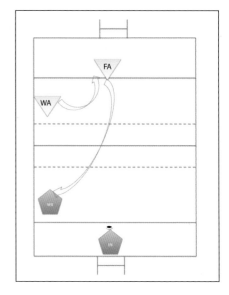

CHAPTER 7 – DEFENCE

This chapter contains the following drills designed to develop skills in defence.

CHAPTER 7

Defence

In the pre-match build-up before England played Samoa in an autumn international some years ago, former England centre and current Sky Sports rugby pundit, Will Greenwood, admitted that even when he was playing for his country, the first thing he noticed on the field was how big his opposition were. He said it didn't affect the way he played but the thought still crossed his mind.

Many people still believe that defence is all about big hits and driving aggressive contact skills – it really isn't. Many teams do believe that smashing through a defensive line is the way to bring success in attack; the reality is that most coaches spend their time looking at ways of creating or seeking out space to put players through a space in a defensive line. With that knowledge in mind, isn't it fair to assume that defence should be about ensuring that the spaces in your defence are held to a minimum?

This chapter doesn't just give you activities to help make the tackles that you need to defend your goal-line, it also has activities that support the basic tenets of defensive play that are sometimes forgotten:

■ Communication
■ Organization
■ Singular movement
■ Confident tackling

It's wonderful that you have a player in your team who is regarded as the finest tackler of his peer group but if that player is constantly in the wrong place organizationally, he cannot use those hard-earned skills when it really matters; this chapter will give you many activities that you can work on with your team to bring about a successful and energetic defensive policy.

BASIC DEFENSIVE MOVEMENT (1)

How do you get all players to move at the same time? The next few drills will help with this problem.

How it works
Fig. 7.1 Create two channels with cones that are 5m apart – can be as long as you require. Four players stand at the start of one channel.

Fig. 7.2 On coach's call, the four players jog to the first line and stop, readjust their feet to ensure they are 'onside'. This continues until they have gone up and down the channels and returned to the start.

To increase difficulty
■ Make the players start every line in a push-up position.
■ Increase the distances between the cones.

Fig. 7.1

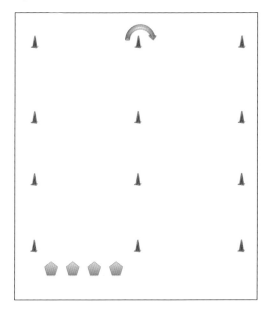

Fig. 7.2

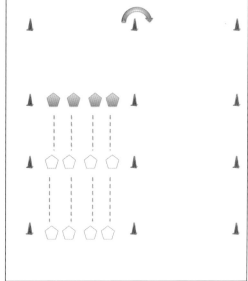

BASIC DEFENSIVE MOVEMENT (2)

How it works
Fig. 7.3   As with the first movement drill, create two channels with cones that are 5m apart – can be as long as you require. Four players stand at the start of one channel.

Fig. 7.4   On coach's call, the four players jog to the first line and stop, readjust their feet to ensure they are 'onside'. Another four players join the line that group has just left. This time, the call is made by a chosen player on the start line, at which point all lines have to start their forward movement. This continues until every team of four has gone up and down the channels and returned to the start.

To increase difficulty
■ Make the players start every line in a push-up position.
■ Increase the distances between the cones.

Note: the person who makes the call to move forward will begin their run slightly ahead of their team mates due to reaction time. Ensure the caller waits for the rest of the team before moving forward. This coaching point will aid doglegs close to a breakdown in match play.

Fig. 7.3

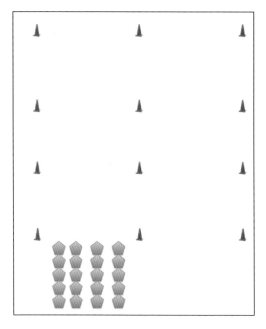

Fig. 7.4

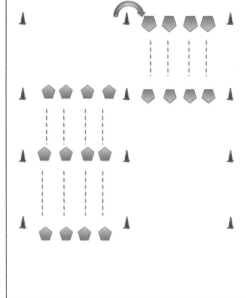

BASIC DEFENSIVE MOVEMENT (3)

How it works

Fig. 7.5 Set up in a similar fashion to the previous two drills; this time the pattern involves some lateral movement.

Fig. 7.6 When the players reach the first set of cones, they move sideways as a team and realign for movement up the second channel. They can do this as individual teams of four or as a team exercise where one caller leads the whole activity – an amalgamation of both previous drills. Continue until they reach the end of the channel and sprint back to the start.

To increase difficulty
- Increase the distances between the cones.
- Place a five-second time limit on realignment – reduce as experience grows.

Fig. 7.5

Fig. 7.6

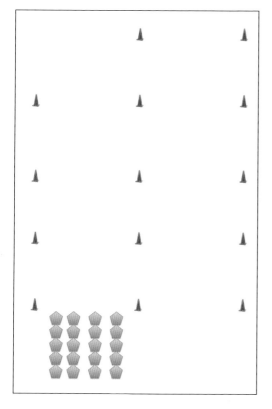

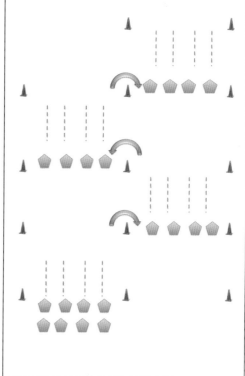

THE BUTTERCUP (1)

Although this is quite time-consuming to set up, once your players understand the key concepts, it allows you to work with a large number of players at once while setting them challenges with increasing complexity. This drill is a trust exercise to show that even if you can't see the player on your own team, when they call, you must move forward together.

How it works
Fig. 7.7   Ask each player to work with a partner – there is no contact in this drill so size doesn't matter. Number the players 1 and 2. All of the player 1s stand shoulder to shoulder making a circle – the players face outwards. All of the player 2s stand opposite their partner but 10m away. If looked at overhead, it would be two circles of players facing each other.

Fig. 7.8   The coach stands on the outside of the two circles with a ball in their hand. When the coach raises the ball in the air, those players that can see shout 'ready'. When the coach drops the ball the players that can see shout 'up' and they touch their partners on their shoulders and jog back. The coach then continues this drill while walking around the outside raising and lowering the ball.

Fig. 7.7

Fig. 7.8

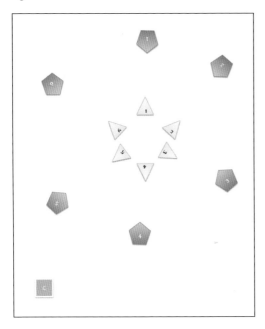

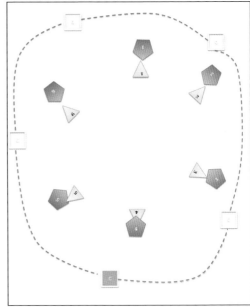

THE BUTTERCUP (2)

Once you are happy with the team's movement – synchronized and suitably vocal – try this to make them engage their brains that little bit more.

How it works
Fig. 7.9 Similar to the previous drill, this time the players will be leaving their assigned partners. To highlight this, I have assigned the partners a matching number.

Fig. 7.10 This time, when the coach raises the ball in the air and the players that can see them shout 'ready' the coach gives a further instruction: this time, the coach adds a number and a direction. In our example, the coach has shouted 'one – right'. This means that all the players on the smaller circle must move around the circle one place to their right, which means that the person they are defending against has changed.

To ensure that every outside defender is now being 'marked up', every player on the inside has to indicate to the players either side of them that they are covering a certain player by pointing at them. The coach then drops the ball and if any player has made a mistake, it should become clear very quickly to the coach.

To increase difficulty
■ Increase the number of movements to the left or right.

Fig. 7.9

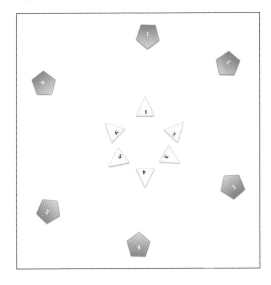

Fig. 7.10

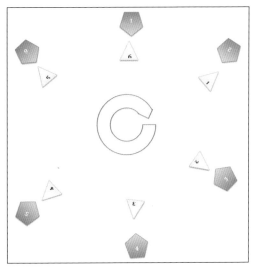

TACKLE TUBE (1)

Many coaches simply use tackle tubes as something that need to be hit, usually very hard with little technical ability. However, tackle tubes can be as valuable as any piece of equipment in your school/club locker if you look at them with a little imagination. Try the next few drills to spark your imagination.

How it works
Fig. 7.11   Five tackle tubes face three players – coach stands behind the tubes.

Fig. 7.12   When the coach shouts 'go', the players run out and tackle the tube directly opposite them. If the coach places their left or right arm out, every player moves one place in that direction and tackles that particular tube. In our example, the coach points to the players' right and they all move across one place to the right and tackle that tube.

To increase difficulty
■ Let the players begin their run but delay the direction – this will highlight that forward movement first is key in defence.

Fig. 7.11

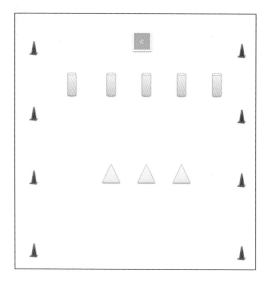

Fig. 7.12

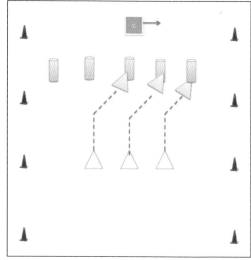

TACKLE TUBE (2)

Sometimes a ball becomes loose in the tackle…

How it works
Fig. 7.13   Three tackle tubes face five players. The coach stands behind the tubes with a ball. The coach will again point a direction (see previous drill).

Fig. 7.14   The coach asks the players to tackle the tubes in the direction he is pointing which means at all times there will be three players working and two that are free. Once the tubes have been tackled, the coach throws a ball in any direction. One of the two free players dives on the ball and pops it up to the other free player to score over a try line behind the coach.

Fig. 7.13

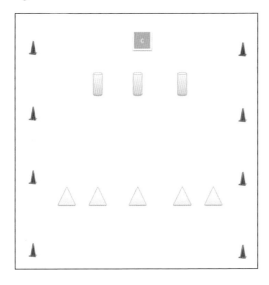

Fig. 7.14

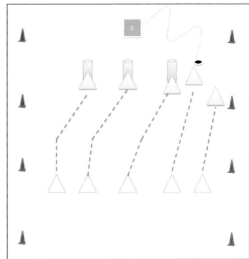

PREVENTING THE OFFLOAD (1)

In defence, once a teammate has completed a tackle, it is important that you get to that person to either steal the ball from the player they have tackled, counter-ruck, tackle a player who has just received an offload, or simply provide close-in defence to allow your team to realign and reset after this phase of play. Try this drill to start that process.

How it works

Fig. 7.15 Have two tackle tubes, with two lines of players standing about 10m away. The coach stands behind the tube.

Fig. 7.16 Coach calls 'up' and both players act as if they are tackling the tube in front of them. Almost immediately, the coach calls either 1 or 2. The number called is the tube that needs to be hit but the player on the other tube must get to that bag as fast as possible and place a hand on it. In our example, the coach calls 'up – 2'.

Fig. 7.15

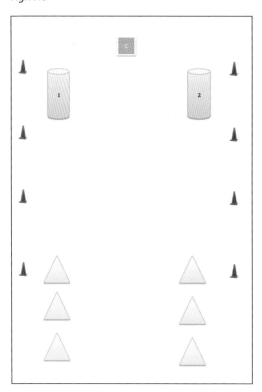

Fig. 7.16

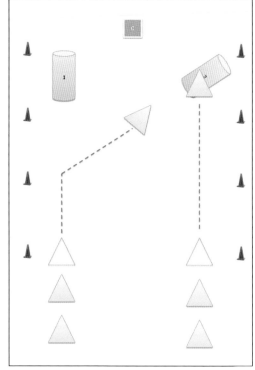

PREVENTING THE OFFLOAD (2)

This drill requires that both players arrive at the tackle tube at the same time.

How it works

Fig. 7.17   Set up is similar to the previous drill – two tackle tubes, two lines of players – but this time the lines are in the centre of the channel and not facing the tubes.

Fig. 7.18   On coach's call, the first arriving player must tackle low and the other must tackle high. Based on your own defensive ideas, you may wish to reverse this. In our example, the coach calls 'up – 2', B went low as A went high.

Fig. 7.17

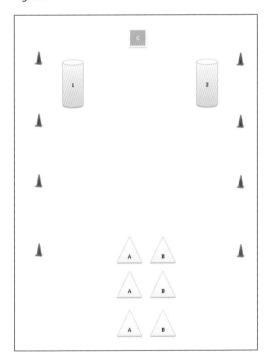

Fig. 7.18

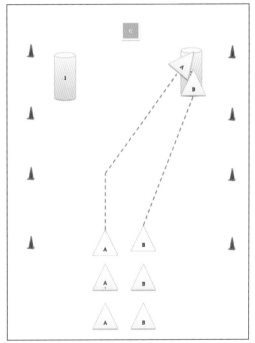

HEAD PLACEMENT

In the modern game, more and more injuries are occurring due to players placing their heads poorly in a tackle. Although very basic in nature, you will be surprised how many players will get their head placement wrong as the tempo increases. In matches, changes in direction by the ball carrier mean that each player has to recognize that their initial thoughts on head placement may now be ineffective.

How it works
Fig. 7.19 In a 10m × 10m box, place five players. Four of the players stand about 3m from a player in the middle. Each of these players is numbered 1, 2, 3 or 4. Each of the numbered players puts their hands out in front of them as if they were actually holding a ball (unless you have enough balls for every player). The numbered players can face any direction they wish.

Fig. 7.20 The coach shouts a number and the player in the middle simply runs towards the relevant player placing his head on the correct side and wrapping his arms around that player. Then return to the centre to await the next number. They do not tackle any player. Repeat this as many times as necessary.

Note: the tackler needs to approach every player as if they were tackling them and put their head in the appropriate way to safely execute that tackle based on how the player puts their body (turned, front to them, back to them and so on). Also, ask your team to ensure the player is placing their head correctly – it is in their interests to ensure correct technique also.

To increase difficulty
■ Decrease the time between each number called so the player has to think on their feet and put their head in the right place and return to the middle before the next number is called.

Fig. 7.19

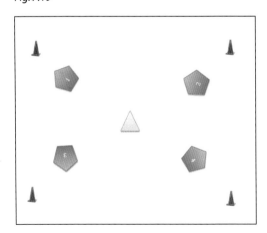

Fig. 7.20

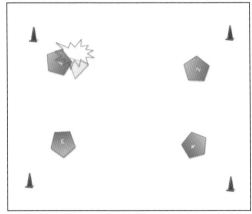

TACKLE PYRAMID

Confidence in tackling is a key component of helping young players feel safe when playing rugby. This drill is designed to help each player adapt their bodies to tackling while allowing you to see where their skill level currently lies – also allowing you to intervene should there be any problems.

How it works
Fig. 7.21 Create a grid 5m × 5m. Have one player with a ball stand on one side of the grid and have one player in the centre facing them – kneeling on their right knee, with their right arm out to the side.

Fig. 7.22 The ball carrier tries to score a try at the far end of the grid but must go through the outstretched arm of the player kneeling – no hand offs or side steps allowed. Each journey across the grid is progressively more difficult. The ball carrier must make five tackles on the ball carrier while they:

- Walk across
- Walk across more quickly
- Jog across
- Jog across more quickly (75 per cent of running pace)
- Run across

Then once both have tackled on their right, they change to the left-hand side.

Note: the first two tackles will give the kneeling player confidence knowing that the harder ones are to come.

To increase difficulty
- Have two ball carriers with a defender taking a tackle on the right and then on the left.

Fig. 7.21

Fig. 7.22

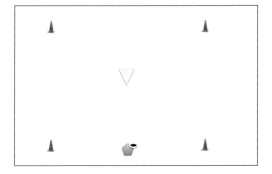

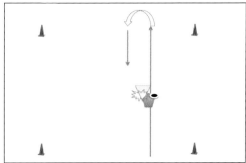

THE SLIDE DEFENCE

Although good teams should always score with overlaps available, why make it easy for them? Try this drill to rehearse your slide defence when you are outnumbered.

How it works
Fig. 7.23   Set up a 25m × 20m channel. Four attackers stand at one end of the channel while 5m in front of them are two defenders.

Fig. 7.24   Once the coach has started the activity, ask the defenders to slide diagonally backwards with the outside defender staying on the ball carrier – the inside defender covers a pass back inside.

To increase difficulty
- Increase the activity area to place the defenders under more pressure.
- Place several sets of four at either end of the channel and the activity can be a continuous exercise for the two defenders.

Note: ideally you would want to defend by moving forward and tackling aggressively but when outnumbered, sliding the attack towards the touchline by sacrificing territory is sometimes necessary.

Fig. 7.23

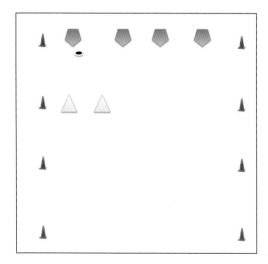

Fig. 7.24

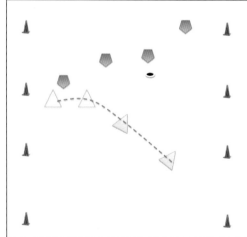

DEFENDING IN THREES

This drill will help your defenders to work with their colleagues to the left and right to ensure a strong defensive line whilst running across the field to chase an attack.

How it works

Fig. 7.25 Working within the 22m area, place two cones 5m out from the posts. Place another cone on the intersection between the 22m and the 15m line and do the same on the other side of the field. Place three players between the posts facing towards the 22m line. Place a ball carrier and two others directly opposite them on the 22m line. When you shout 'go', the attackers on the 22m line decide to run left or right along the 22m line until they reach the cone.

Fig. 7.26 The three attackers then straighten up and attempt to score a try. While the attack is running across the 22m, the three defenders must run out to the cones in front of them and 'slide' across the field ensuring that the three players stay as a unit allowing all of them a good position to defend their try line.

To increase difficulty
■ You can place the cones along the 22m line closer to the attackers to allow them to set up earlier and attack the line – thereby reducing the time the defence has to organize.

Fig. 7.25

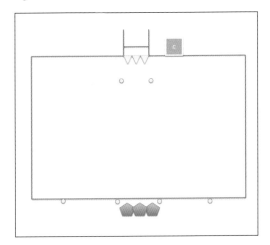

Fig. 7.26

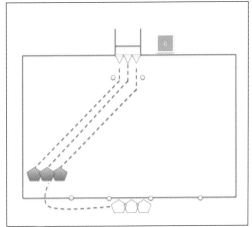

129

TACKLING FATIGUE

This drill will help your tacklers condition their bodies for tackling and getting to their feet quickly to challenge for the ball or tackle again.

How it works
Fig. 7.27   Seven players carrying balls stand at various points on the outside of a 10m × 10m grid. In the middle of the grid is a defender. The coach numbers each ball carrier.

Fig. 7.28   When the coach calls a number (in our example, the coach called the number 3), that player runs to the side of the grid directly facing where they currently stand. When the tackler has completed a tackle, they get to their feet and the coach calls another number and so on. The previously tackled player continues the run across the grid.

Once the tackler reaches their personal fatigue level, change the defender.

To increase difficulty
■ If you have a particularly strong tackler, push them to make positive tackles only, i.e. tackles where the ball carrier does not gain any ground following the tackle and is driven back to their starting point.

Note: be aware that a fatigued tackler can become a poor tackler and therefore care needs to be taken as the end result of poor tackle technique due to fatigue may be injury.

Fig. 7.27

Fig. 7.28

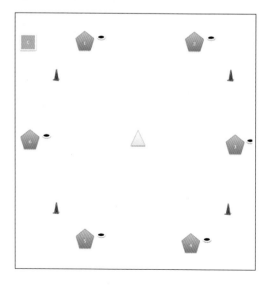
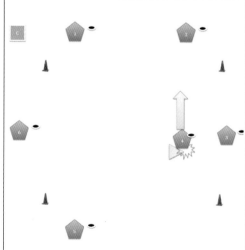

PENETRATING RUNNER

Following on from covering a defender 1-on-1, what happens in a defensive line when the opposition put a runner into the line that hasn't been accounted for? This drill will begin that process of trying to deal with this eventuality.

How it works
Fig. 7.29 Place four tubes, 15m in front of a line of four players. Number the spaces between the tubes. Behind the tackle tubes have a player with a tackle shield. The coach stands behind the four defenders. On the left hand side of the chan-nel, place three or four tackle shields to signify a breakdown. (Whatever your defensive pattern is, it is usually based on where the breakdown is, hence the placement of the tackle shields – it aids the players in defence.)

Figs. 7.30 and 7.31 On the coach's call, the four players run to tackle the tubes. When the line has started, the coach holds up a number of fingers to signal which space he wants the penetrating runner to enter. In our example, the player enters space number 2. All players then adjust accordingly based on your particular defensive pattern.

To increase difficulty
■ Bring the defenders closer to the tubes.
■ Have two penetrating runners.

Fig. 7.29

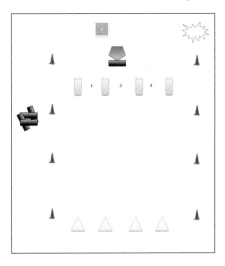

Fig. 7.30

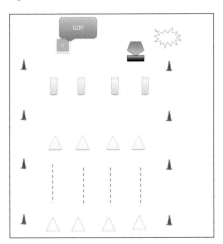

Fig. 7.31

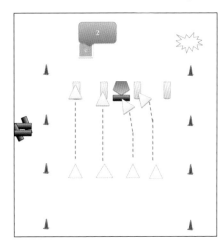

SCRAMBLE TACKLE

Scramble tackles are used when your opponent would run outside you if you didn't change your angle of approach. Try this drill to begin the path to great scramble tackling.

How it works
Fig. 7.32 Set up two start lines approximately 10m apart. On the defence side of the grid, place a series of 'gates' that the ball carrier needs to run through. Also have a mini-channel 5m long in front of the defender.

Fig. 7.33 When the coach calls a number, the ball carrier must run straight to that 'gate'. The defender runs the length of the mini-channel and then changes direction to make the tackle. Depending on the number called, the tackle requires more scrambling to get there.
In our example, the coach called number 1.

To increase difficulty
■ Reduce the space between the ball carrier and the 'gates'.
■ Run forwards against back and vice versa – create mismatches and see what happens.

Note: ideally, the 'gates' should be made from agility poles but cones will allow the drill to work equally well.

Fig. 7.32

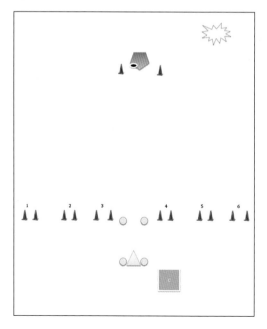

Fig. 7.33

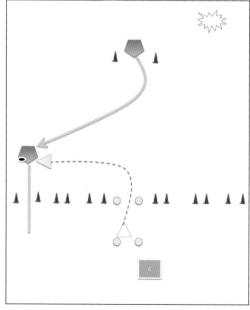

CONTINUOUS DEFENCE DRILL

There is a book to be written about what a coach can do when they turn up at the field to see they only have a few players at training. We have all been to training when you have fewer than ten players to work with, a mixture of backs and forwards and, in all probability, falling temperatures to deal with too. This activity is one of my favourites when discussing how to work with a partner in defence.

How it works
Fig. 7.34   Create two 20m × 15m channels side by side. Have three to six players as attackers and two as defenders.

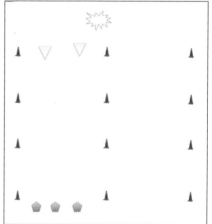

Fig. 7.34

Fig. 7.35   The three attackers try to score at the end of the first channel against the two defenders. If they are successful, they continue around the end of that channel into the next. The defenders have complete freedom to run any defence pattern they wish to try and stop the three attackers. If the defence succeed, then simply run through and realign in the next channel. The key to the defence is to pressure the attack as much as possible by rushing up the channel before the attack has a chance to organize.

To increase difficulty
Fig. 7.36
- If you believe all defenders have learned the lessons, change the activity by removing the cones that divide the channels and try the activity across the full width as a 5 vs. 3 continuous drill.

Fig. 7.36

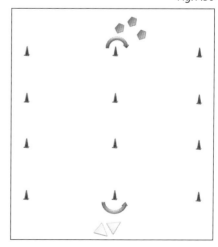

Fig. 7.35

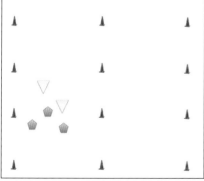

TEACH THE BLITZ (NON-CONTACT)

A Blitz style of defence is much as it sounds – you sprint up onto the player you are marking as quickly as possible to close down the space and reduce their thinking time in the hope of errors in attack being made. It has its positives and negatives but if having done your research you feel this is an area you could develop, here is a drill to help.

How it works
Fig. 7.37 Use a line already on the field as a try line. Place five cones of differing colour on the floor facing this line, set up as if they were an attacking back line. Have five players stand on the line facing the five cones.

Fig. 7.38 On coach's call each player runs out, touches the cone and stays. On coach's second call, all players return to the line.

Fig. 7.39 Once players are happy to see how the drill works, coach calls again but then follows it with a colour once the line starts the run (in our example, 'go ... red!'). This is to simulate a tackle made by a defender that the rest have to react to. Once the defensive line reaches the cone of that colour, the line stops and realigns on that cone. Then return back to the line.

Fig. 7.37

To increase difficulty
- Increase the 'depth' of the cones. This will make the distance covered by the players from the line more realistic.
- Increase the spacing between the cones.

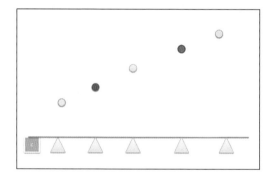

Fig. 7.38

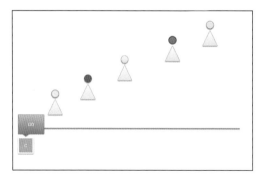

Fig. 7.39

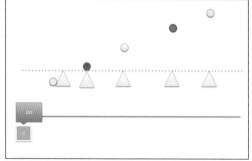

RABBIT OUT OF THE LINE

In defence, if you can stop a wide attack before it has even begun to be exploited by your opposition, it is something you should try to look at if you believe the players' experience levels could make this a reality. This drill will help you start the process of building a new facet into your defensive strategy.

How it works

Play a game of touch rugby with an attacking back line of seven players versus five in defence – a game that has an overlap on every occasion. To begin with, play between the 15m lines on a full-sized pitch but expand once defenders start to understand their roles.

Fig. 7.40 Once you have played a few phases, instruct the third man from the breakdown to sprint out of the line at his opposite number every time the ball is passed by their 9.

Fig. 7.41 (Although the defensive line moves forward, this player would sprint out faster than his team mates, leaving them behind.) The defence then reacts to what happens next – it may be a long pass out wide, a pass back inside or a hit up.

Note: after a few minutes of doing this, it may be worth seeing if the players could run the system themselves and not run up every time – only when it was necessary to stop the ball going wide.

Fig. 7.40

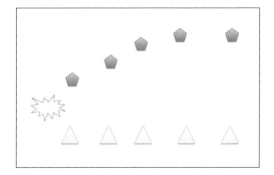

Fig. 7.41

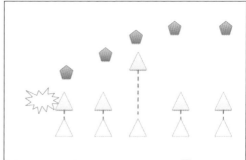

CHASING A LONG KICK

One of the many areas of concern for any team is the number of times poor kicks are not followed down the field with effective chasing. You can get away with a bad kick down the field but unless someone organizes a pressurizing chase, then it becomes a significant counter-attack opportunity for a good attacking back three. Try this drill to see if it helps.

How it works
Fig. 7.42 Working in the area between the 22m line, place a full back on one 22m line and three defenders on the other 22m line. Ask a player to kick the ball to the full back.

Fig. 7.43 This starts the three defenders chasing as a single line. The middle of the three chasing players (number 2) must stay on the ball carrier while the other two prevent them from running around the outside or side-stepping the middle player.

To increase difficulty
■ Have two attackers run the ball back.

Fig. 7.42

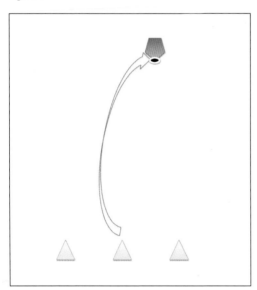

Fig. 7.43

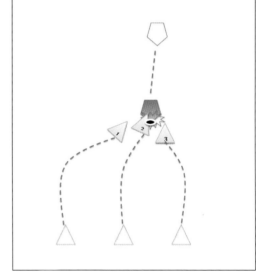

WORKING IN PAIRS

This drill is based not so much around making the tackle but how to assist a colleague who has already made contact with a ball carrier.

How it works
Fig. 7.44   Set up a 15m × 10m channel. Have one attacker and one defender facing each other. Place one attacker and one defender on the side of the channel ready to enter the game.

Fig. 7.45   The defender tries to stop a ball carrier from beating him in a channel. Once the defender makes contact (not necessarily a 'tackle') the second defender and the second attacker enter the game. It is the work of the second defender you are watching – do they focus on the ball or focus on the defender?

To increase difficulty
■ Bring all players into the channel (2 vs. 2) and continue. This will reduce the space for the attack and therefore should make defending it easier. However, the action will now happen more dynamically and at a much higher pace.

Fig. 7.44

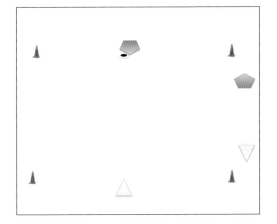

Fig. 7.45

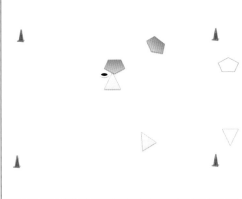

THE TWO-MAN TACKLE (1)

A drill to help your players make a two-man tackle, giving them a better chance to make more dynamic and confident tackle line engagements.

How it works
Fig. 7.46   Create a 10m × 10m grid. On one side of the grid place a ball carrier and on the opposite side, two defenders.

Fig. 7.47   The ball carrier starts with the ball in two hands and jogs towards the two defenders. When within 3m of the defenders, they 'tuck' the ball close to their body with one arm. The defender on the side where the ball is held with one arm tackles at chest height 'above' or 'on' the ball. The defender on the opposite side of the ball hits low and drives the ball carrier backwards or sideways. This will prevent an offload and may lead to a 'choke' tackle.

To increase difficulty
■ Increase the speed of the ball carrier.

Fig. 7.46

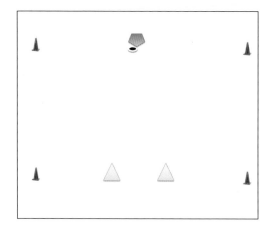

Fig. 7.47

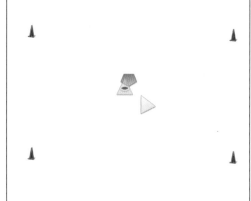

THE TWO-MAN TACKLE (2)

Although having the ability to tackle an attacker with two defenders is ideal, what happens if the ball carrier has a support runner? This drill will start that learning process.

How it works

Fig. 7.48   Create a 10m × 10m grid. On one side of the grid place a ball carrier and on the opposite side, two defenders.

Fig. 7.49   All of the steps to make a two-man tackle in the previous drill apply here; however, with the addition of the second attacker, the defender 'marking' the ball carrier needs to decide whether:

- They tackle low to bring the defender to the ground.
- Tackle high in the hope their defending partner can support them.
- Both defenders commit to the ball carrier leaving a free attacker in space to receive a ball should the defence get the call wrong.

Fig. 7.48

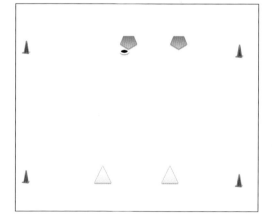

Fig. 7.49

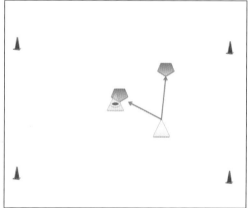

TACKLE VARIETY GAME

When training, it is difficult to replicate actual match play especially in defence as the intensity and the variety of tackles made in an average rugby game varies so dramatically from contact to contact. This drill will make your players think about whom they are tackling and with what technique.

How it works
Fig. 7.50   Have two equal teams play a full contact game within the 22m area – width to be determined by the coach. On three of the players in attack, place three different coloured bibs. The three colours relate to the types of tackle that must be made on them. In our example:

■ A RED player must be tackled below the knees.
■ A YELLOW player must be tackled at chest height.
■ A BLUE player must be tackled using the two-man tackle technique.

After five minutes of constant attack, change the players in the bibs or give the ball to the other team who have their own bibs. All other players in attack can be tackled as they would in a normal game as the rules regarding the colours only apply to those in bibs.

Fig. 7.50

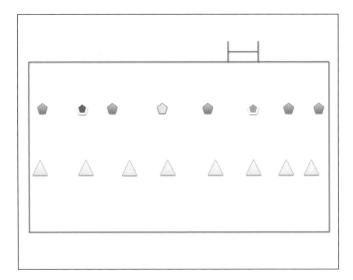

RANDOM DEFENCE PLAY

If you do not have thirty players in your squad but wish to play a competitive game, clever use of shields and tubes can allow your players to stay out rucks and work on their open play attack and defence skills.

How it works
Fig. 7.51   At random points around the field, place shields and tubes to simulate a ruck. Place cones down to show the back of each ruck (this helps with offside lines). Number each ruck on the field. Create two teams – appoint one as the attack. Every time the coach calls a colour, all players must realign on that ruck. After 5 seconds, allowing the attack and the defence to organize, start the play and allow each team to run their best attack or defence as they wish. After one phase, coach should change the number of the ruck and the game begins again.

To increase difficulty
■ Lower the time each team has to prepare before restarting the play.
■ Overload the attack over the defence making the defence change their pattern to adapt.

Fig. 7.51

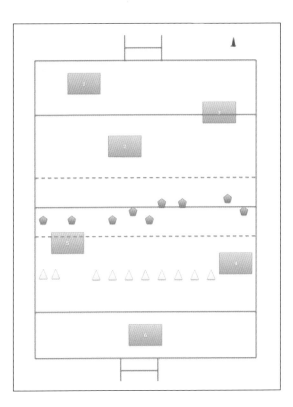

CHAPTER 8 – SPEED UP THE GAME

This chapter contains the following drills designed to develop players' speed.

Quick 22-Metre Drop Out

Quick Line-Out

Quick Restart

Free Kick From Scrum

High Catch and Pass

Speed Up The Game

Nothing strikes fear into a team's defence than an opposition player doing something that they simply didn't expect. As players mature, the space available to them becomes more difficult to exploit as defensive patterns have become so well organized even at the lowest ends of the game. Therefore striking, while the defence is still in a state of flux, is something that we should really try to do more often.

It is hoped that the drills that follow will allow you to come up with your own ideas about where you can take advantage of a situation when the opposition is still considering what has happened previously.

When I am asked about the best ways to exploit defences, I always throw a question back to the coach: 'To which side of the field do you kick off?' Often they say they kick off to the left; most teams do. The ones that have variety in their kick offs are coaches who have spent some time considering who they have in their team, what their strengths are and have wondered, can they get the ball back from the kick off by being cleverer than their opponents?

As I say in the introduction to the chapter on kicking, giving the ball to the opposition to run back at you is usually a bad idea, so try and get it back as soon as you can. There are many areas of the game you can look at and although coaching players to use their imagination early on will cause problems for you, in the long term, your team will be the most imaginative and joyous teams to watch in your area.

QUICK 22-METRE DROP OUT

The first thing many attacking teams do when the ball is touched down behind their opponents' posts is to run to the middle of the 22m line – that's where they feel the drop out will automatically happen.

How it works

Fig. 8.1   Using the 22m area, create two teams. Using the areas on the field highlighted in Fig. 1, ask one player to get the ball, touch it down and ensure there is a player at each of areas shown. Throw the ball behind the goal and a player touches the ball down for a 22m drop out.

Fig. 8.2   That player must immediately throw (or kick) the ball to area 1. Which area 1 depends on which side of the posts the ball was touched down. Once the ball gets to area 1, that person tries to complete a quick drop out to themselves. If the opposition has covered that option, immediately throw the ball to area 2.

If area 2 is covered throw the ball to area 3 where there are three players standing. Usually for 22m drop outs, the opposition place two players to cover a drop out so by having three, you may have an opportunity to complete a very short drop kick which you my be able to retain due to your greater numbers. If all options are covered, then complete your normal drop out procedure.

Note: if everyone on your team is aware that quick drop outs are an option, the players with the ball can drop out to themselves and then pass the ball back between their legs to start a counter-attack.

Fig. 8.1

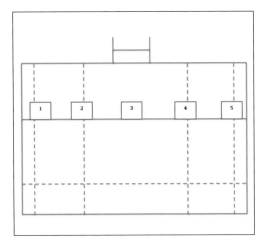

Fig. 8.2

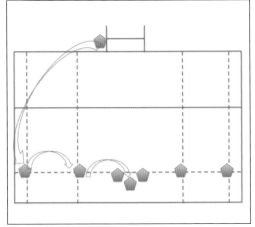

QUICK LINE-OUT

When the opposition decides to kick a ball down the field, they often sacrifice putting the ball several metres into touch to gain an advantage in distance. This opens up an opportunity for you to start a possible counter-attack so to help look at this area, try this drill.

How it works
Fig. 8.3 Place a ball in touch at the 22m line. Have three attackers stand on the 10m line with a defender on the furthest 10m line.

Fig. 8.4 On the coach's call, one player runs to the ball, a second runs to the 5m line and the third stands about 20m away from where the ball is about to be thrown in. All decisions about who should receive the ball are based on where the defender runs to – either in-field or towards the 5m line.

To increase difficulty
■ Add more players in attack and defence.
■ Make the players chasing the ball pick it up while it is still moving.

Fig. 8.3

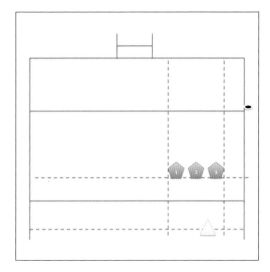

Fig. 8.4

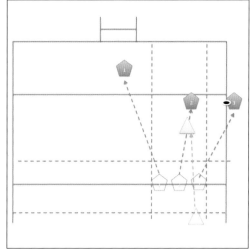

QUICK RESTART

In a close game when time is running out, a quick half-way restart following a try against you is something you may wish to do, but how can you stack the odds of retrieving the ball in your favour?

How it works
Fig. 8.5   Have the 9 and 10 stand about 10m behind the posts to catch the ball (further if allowed). Beforehand, have one prop, one second row and one back row designated to run to the half-way line on the right- or left-hand side.

Fig. 8.6   Once the kick has been made, the ball must get to the 10 but the 10 must sprint to the half-way line. Whoever catches the ball must get the ball to the 9 who then ensures the ball gets to the 10. The designated forwards join the wingers in offering up two sides of the field for a possible chase. The kicker chooses the side least well defended by scanning what's in front of them as they run down the field to the half-way line.

Fig. 8.5

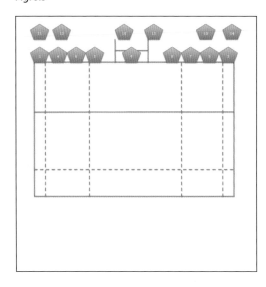

Fig. 8.6

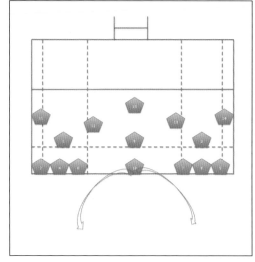

FREE KICK FROM SCRUM

For a variety of offences, a scrum free kick maybe given in your favour. Depending on your field position, you may wish to immediately tap and go, as any delay would allow the opposition to organize their defensive pattern. This is one way to rehearse that moment.

How it works
Fig. 8.7   Place two tackle tubes on the floor and have your flankers place their inside arm onto it and the 8 places both hands at the rear of the tubes. A 9 stands at the front of the tubes with a ball in hand. As a back line, a 10, 12 and 13 stand in attack formation.

Fig. 8.8   Coach blows the whistle and the 9 throws the ball to the 8. The 8 taps and runs to where he believes the opposition's first defender would be. Your 12 runs an in line to act as a distracting runner. Before contact, the 8 passes the ball to the out running 10 who has 13 in support.

To increase difficulty
■ Add more defenders plus an attacking 15.

Fig. 8.7

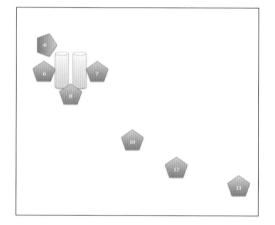

Fig. 8.8

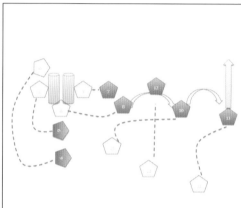

HIGH CATCH AND PASS

With the full back looking up into the air at a falling ball, unless they receive clear instructions, it is difficult for them to react to anything that is happening around them. This drill allows the coach to help the full back catch the ball but also create a support structure around the full back from supporting players to create possible counter-attack scenarios.

How it works
Fig. 8.9   Place a full back inside the 22m line. A support runner (S) on the 22m line and a chasing attacker (C) with a tackle shield. Finally, you need someone to put up high kicks for the full back to catch (K).

Fig. 8.10   Once the kick has been made, the support runner runs behind the catcher. While the ball is in mid-air the catcher communicates with the full back as to whether a counter-attack is on or whether they should call a 'mark'. The support player should also be aware of whether the full back is taking the ball standing still or running onto it (the latter being a good way to start a counter-attack if it is in a positive direction). The coach decides how much contact the shield-holder should make on the full back.

To increase difficulty
■ The kicker chases the support runner.

Fig. 8.9

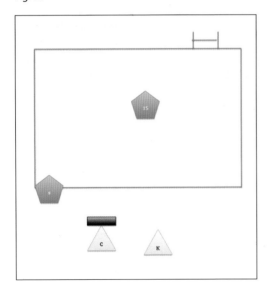

Fig. 8.10

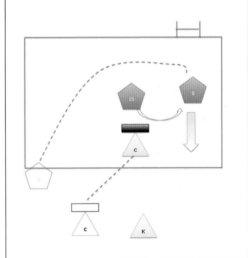

CHAPTER 9

Questions About The Game

Over the last number of years, I have been honoured to write for several publications about the rugby game from the view of a coach working with players from U7s to senior internationals, both in the UK and overseas. I have tried with these articles to pass along some thoughts I have on the game but also express the thoughts of the many thousands of people I have met in the game over the years and who have been kind enough to let me watch them work.

The following articles are just a handful of the many I have written but I felt that these would be particularly appropriate for this book, with thoughts on how taking a different view can lead a team to a more innovative approach to their play.

THE CARDINAL RULES OF AMATEUR RUGBY COACHING

Don't take credit for a former player's success

As you go through your coaching career, you will undoubtedly meet players who by a twist of fate, genetics or some other intangible are something very special indeed. They will bring to the table something that will allow them, if developed correctly, to become a player who later performs at the highest level. Along their path, you will inevitably give them some little titbits to see them go in a better direction but overall, their own

personal ambition has got them to where they are at the moment.

I have coached players currently playing at various levels all over the world. Some in the Premiership/Championship in England, Top 14 in France, NPC in New Zealand and for the USA National teams. However, I am not responsible for their success and I would never dare suggest that even though they play at those levels, I should live off their names. You may very well have been an important part of their life but that is for them to announce to the world, not you. You can take pride that you knew them and that you played a valued and very important part in their young development as a rugby player, but to deny that they are where they are because of their hard work is a little insulting. And it may be the case that the player doesn't feel the same about you…!

Never 'bad mouth' another amateur coach

It is hard work being a coach. You are constantly being compared to the standards set on television by professional coaches even though you have a 'paid' job to do before you start your evening coaching position. In a similar way to actors, there are very few professional coaching jobs; those that have them tend to be good at it as they have the time to invest in their own personal success. However, as an amateur, every waking moment that isn't invested in family or work is given over to learning more about the rugby game – so why would you spend your time bad mouthing a colleague when you know exactly what they are going through and what sacrifices they have made to be in competition with you on a sporting field? Why waste what little time you have to develop your game and your players on bad mouthing another coach? No good will ever come of it and with social media as it is today, you will never be able to take it back.

Evolve
Reliving past glories is a great way to spend an afternoon by a pool with good friends when you have retired from coaching. It is not a way to make you a better coach. In my time as a coach, I have won and lost many high-profile matches and events. If you ask me, I will tell you what they are but if you don't, I am happy to keep those memories for later life. There is a time and place for highlighting your strengths: on your résumé!

If you are constantly saying you have done this or that, you are leaving no time for you to say where you wish to be. Never being satisfied with the status quo is a good thing, but sometimes, when you want to evolve a process, you will constantly be met by people who are happy to keep things the way they are. It is easier for them to understand something they know than try to take the time to imagine what they don't. There is nothing more nauseating in life than someone who tells you how good they are when they should be telling you how good they could be!!

Your job is to coach players
Players win games; coaches help them. Although many books have been written about Zen and the Art of Coaching, anything that steers away from the premise that you are there to aid a player's development, is not a good read. As children are often a reflection of their parents, the way a team plays is a reflection of you as a coach – so concentrate

on them. Paul 'Bear' Bryant said it best: 'No coach has ever won a game by what he knows – it's what his players know that counts.'

Do your research
You just watched a really exciting rugby game on TV. You take the time to work out a drill or an activity that will help your team replicate a moment in that game you wish to see your team develop. They complete it satisfactorily in training but in a match, it's appalling. You never use it again.

How many times has this happened to you? The reason why it hasn't worked comes to you after a while and it is always followed with a slap to the forehead and an utterance of 'duh'. Just because the best teams in the world can do it, doesn't mean your team can immediately follow suit. You are asking a group of well-intentioned young players to imitate a highly skilled, fully professional team.

Doing your research about not only the skills you have seen, but also the relative skills set of your team in comparison will allow you to look at what you are asking them to do a little more dispassionately. Following this reflection, maybe a pared-down version of the skill or a long-term plan leading to its inclusion in your team's pattern may be the way to go here.

Other people's interests can help you
Every year, I try to look at rugby in a different way. I look at how the game that I coach can be helped by other sports. Recently, athletics and ice hockey are particular study areas but in the past I have looked at golf, volleyball, netball, basketball, soccer and a list of others too lengthy to mention. Although many of the interesting parts of any coaching book are repeated, occasionally, just one line can change the way you think about a subject.

The best coaching book I have ever read is a basketball one. The best rugby management book is Australian, and the biggest influence on my particular specialist coaching area is judo. Many of my successful American rugby colleagues have similar stories and interests and we often pass tips to each other about books/websites we have seen and have learned from. Don't limit yourself.

It is also a positive idea to trawl the parents or other family members of your players to see what they have in their athletic arsenal that they could give to you. It will usually be free and well-meaning, and that person will take a huge amount of pleasure from the experience.

Smile
You chose the game – it didn't choose you. So enjoy yourself. Sometimes, we can forget that.

How long should I spend on a handling session for mini rugby?
If you follow some simple guidelines, the timing of a handling session will become apparent to you as you control the length of time the session takes by setting an achievable target, as opposed to the players dictating it with looks of boredom and apathy.

Is it fun?
Your players and their parents have given up a morning and handed their children over to you. With this comes a responsibility to ensure that they have fun! They must smile and laugh and feel a determination to succeed at whatever task you set them. Handling is a key part of the game and making the learning of the skill fun will allow you to stretch out the length of handling session.

Is it relevant to the game?
Playing fun games will energize the sessions and give you what you need to meet the aforementioned point. However, it is impor-

tant to remember that, if possible, all activities should be related to the rugby game. Communication drills, ball carrying activities and evasion games all can play a major role in getting across to your players vitally important skills .

Handling does not mean simply running out in lines and passing the ball endlessly. Players getting their hands on the ball as many times as possible in a session, getting a feel of the ball and passing that ball along to a friend will allow them to improve their handling.

Are they learning anything new or are they reinforcing the basics?
It is difficult to keep reinventing the wheel but as a mini coach, you have a greater opportunity to teach new things than your peers of older teams, as everything you teach them is new. However, constant reinforcement of previously learned skills is also very important. For you as the coach, if you can set either outcome as your final goal, this will allow you to judge how long the session will take, based on whether they have retained their old knowledge or learned what new skill you have given them sufficiently to move on.

How should I run training on a wet and cold evening?
When you coach for a few years, you begin to realize that the biggest lessons were learned under pressure and when things had an opportunity to not go the way they were planned. One of the way coaches 'earn their stripes' is having to keep the players' attention on nights of inclement weather. Inevitably, winter rain means cold, muddy training areas that can distract players from the lessons you are trying to pass along. Therefore, having looked at the weather forecast, you need to plan a session that meets certain standards

to ensure your players get full value from the evening.

Firstly, the session needs to zip along. If you explain at length about what you are about to do, the players will become cold and distracted. Therefore, this would be a good session to spend reinforcing old messages about tackling and contact generally. New ideas need to be dissected with time set aside should players feel confused or unsure of the outcome required … a wet cold night is not that time!

Secondly, have the player 'conversation breaks' in a place that allows the players to hear what you are saying. Before moving onto a new part of the session, jog the team to a part of the field where there is shelter from the wind, under a tree or even near the clubhouse. Once there, you can discuss your points and answer the players' queries in a location where they can all hear you and, just as importantly, you can hear them.

Finally, make the session shorter than normal. If you are making the session move along faster, with shortened rest periods, then end the session earlier and get them out of the rain and the cold. There is nothing to be gained by keeping them out on the field once the goals for the evening have been achieved.

Nothing warms players up on a cold evening like contact. As the ground is wet, they will have a reluctance to fall to the ground but once they have acclimatized to surroundings, I have always found players thrive on wet evenings and the camaraderie shown at the end is worth a thousand team-building sessions.

How to work on hard grounds

There's a reason why countries with long hot summers play a fast and open style of rugby – they don't like contact on hard grounds

either! In the northern hemisphere, playing matches in September and half of October usually involves playing on hard grounds which, unless you decide to play in a plastic bubble, means your players will need to adjust to contact on hard ground. However, there are ways of mitigating the ill effects in this area with a few simple adjustments.

Talk to your groundsperson

We play rugby, which is a handling game, so why do clubs always want their fields to be like a billiard table all year round? Have a chat with your groundsperson and ask them to keep a significant depth on the grass in the area where your team will be training. You would be surprised how just having a lot of grass to fall on can help with your pre-season injury count. I am not suggesting 3 feet of grass but 3–4 inches would be good.

Use shields to fall on

When you are doing rucking, simply placing a bag on the floor to land on doesn't in any way effect what you are trying to teach. You will also notice that if players land too far to the sides of the shield, their ball placement is affected so although it looks like a simple 'falling on the shield' exercise, the players will soon realize they have to concentrate more fully on their ground work here as they are now falling on a unstable surface as opposed to the relative familiarity of falling on the ground.

It always rains

You will have a plan for your training sessions but do not be so rigid as to stick to a set of plans that goes against the weather conditions. Rain is inevitable in the many rugby countries so complete all of your 'off-the-ground' work when it's dry but when inclement weather is forecast, simply pull out the sessions on contact you had planned for several weeks before and do them now. Adapt and overcome.

The 'third' set piece

I was on tour in Florida in 2009 when I watched the Scotland vs. Wales Five Nations game after a 24-hour delay. We all settled down and while half of us were ordering drinks, Scotland had scored … straight from the kick off!

Over the years, teams have played with the idea of trying to set up mismatches in the way they kick off. Wales used a forwards split system, I remember England once setting up for the kick off by lining up fourteen of their players in one solid white line across the field and chasing the Wilkinson kick off. I also seem to recall Australia setting up behind the kicker and chasing short.

Today, the modern professional game has been able to explore any number of restart variations and it is mostly from the game of sevens where these new ideas seem to come from. It is in this modified version where the most innovative restarts are seen, as the team who has just scored has to return the ball to the opposition. It is how they have dealt with team solutions to these restarts, which makes this facet of the game so interesting.

Now, before we continue, I would like to show you a magic trick. What I want you to do is just for a second, think of the way you set up for kicks off. Have you done it? Okay, now really concentrate on the page and your kick off will appear on the next line.

Your team kicks off to the left!

I am right, aren't I? Most teams do but if you sat down and thought about it, don't most teams you play against also kick off to the left?

In 1996, I attended a lecture at Murrayfield in Scotland where I spent thirty-five minutes being introduced to the many variations of a 22m drop out … thirty-five minutes!! It was among the greatest presentations of anything I have ever seen but I have never seen anyone repeat it since. You may think it's a nothing subject but if you haven't got a plan other than 'chase the kick', then how do you expect to get the ball back?

In 2002, I attended a Level 3 conference in Ireland where former USA and Ireland coach Eddie O'Sullivan said that after we were given a task to complete with a group of players we had to identify three players at all times:

- A playmaker
- A penetrator
- A support runner

For example, if you were to run a switch pass between a 10 and a 12 from a scrum, 10 would be the playmaker, 12 would be the penetrator and 7 would be the support runner.

I don't know if he was being evil or he just wanted to challenge my experience but he really went after me: my task was the kick off. I had five minutes to prepare a practical presentation highlighting the three roles from a kick off. Go on, have a go at it yourself.

Possession of the ball in 7s is paramount and although the same could be said of 15s, it is not as disastrous if the opposition has the ball … or why would we have 'ping-pong' kicking? However, the best practice of any restart/kick off activity you run with your team is to get the ball back.

The importance of the kick off is now at a point that many are now calling it 'The third set piece' – to highlight how important coaches and players now feel about this area of the game.

There are so many different variables to making a restart work that it doesn't sit well with a coach that there is an activity that cannot be broken down into its consistent parts and developed. As with the breakdown, however, you can only control what your team does. You can't control the wind, rain, snow, opposition catchers and so on. The horrible truth is that when the ball leaves your kicker's foot, you may know where the ball is likely to end up due to hours of practice, but you have no control over where the opposition stands or what they do in response to your kick. You can manipulate where the ball goes and try to make the opposition go to a tiled position to make life harder for them but again, once the ball leaves your kicker's foot, there is little you can do until the ball comes down.

In line-outs and scrums, you have a larger degree of control on where the ball goes or how you set your scrum up for the challenges at the engage but the restarts do not allow you the same control over a chosen path.

All of that being said, I would suggest that how your team restarts a game is among the most regularly ignored parts of the game. Although you may practise it, the level of detail that goes into this part of the game is not as closely looked at as say the scrum or the line-out. There are so many controllable and coachable parts to a kick off that reinforcing it at every team run-through should be a matter of policy.

If you possess the ball, players should know:

- Who is kicking the ball
- Where the ball is going to land
- On which side of the field
- Who is chasing the kick
- Who stays back in case the ball is kicked back

If the ball is being kicked to you, the team should know:

- Who are the most effective receivers
- What is a player's role if a given event happens (e.g. catch near them)
- Who makes the clearing kick if required

- Who are the receivers if a counter-attack can be launched from their poor kick

The 'third set piece' is a phrase you will hear a lot more in the future.

WHAT NOT TO SAY AT HALF TIME

As a coach of a midi side, you have no more than five minutes at half time to get your point across – one minute is taken up getting the players to come to you and another one letting them drink water. With such a short time period available, you must get your points across clearly and efficiently, in the hope of changing the behaviour of your team for the second half.

Don't focus solely on the team's poor play
Of course you need to address parts of your team's performance that are causing issues on the field, but what players need from you is perspective. You have seen what's going wrong, you have an idea how it can be resolved and you need to use half time to help them provide a solution. If all of your feedback is highlighting the negative, what will their frame of mind be for the second half?

Don't personalize
Half time is a team moment. Errors by individuals need to be addressed in training, as there is little you can do to help solve their personal issues in a five-minute talk. Also, if you focus too much on one player, you will de-motivate them, create a 'martyr' for the team and waste very valuable time for other areas to be discussed.

Don't become a cartoon character
Cartoons are at their funniest when they say something inappropriate or are massive exag-

gerations of normal human behaviour. If you say something at half time that you would be very embarrassed to have repeated back to you later, don't say it. This also includes becoming a person who could make themself heard three fields away. You will inadvertently motivate the opposition when they hear you tearing into your team.

Don't bring the mood down

This is a broad point and although it may relate to the first point above, it's to do with reading the players' body language. If they have a positive frame of mind walking to you, don't bring the mood down. There is a fine line between bringing the team back from an over-confident stance and de-motivating them. In essence, re-focus on the pre-match points, state the positives and let them play.

How to use 5 minutes at half time effectively

You cannot teach new ideas to your team in five short minutes unless it is something so blindingly obvious that revealing it will transform everything … trust me, those moments are as rare as chickens' teeth. Therefore, having a plan for the half-time talk is essential. Every good coach has a plan but many feel that five minutes is too short a time to make any real difference.

The following are some ideas if you are a single coach working on your own with a team on match day. (If you have two or more coaches, then times can be adjusted.)

- Time
- Start a stopwatch as soon as the whistle goes for half time. Then confirm with the referee that you actually have five minutes on the field for half time. By asking the referee this question, you are relaying the fact that you are timing half time and you desire all of that time.

- Minute 1: rehydrate
- Your team will not listen to you if they are looking for water, so let them hydrate and say nothing for the first minute. It will seem like a waste of time but it puts their needs first and allows you time to gather your thoughts.
- Minutes 2–4: focused comments
- If your issues are with the forwards, leave the backs with the water and take the forwards a few metres away and talk to them. The backs will not listen to you as it's not relevant to them and having a focused chat with the problem area will make it more directed and relevant. The reverse is also true.
- Minute 5: team issues
- To bring half time to a conclusion, give the team one thing that they need to focus on right from the start of the half. Any more and it will be lost in a haze. You may have ten things to mention and they may still have serious issues in the game but you need to give them an achievable target in the second half and encourage them to work on that one area. The team may not be happy with the overall outcome but if they achieve that one target, your post-game talk will leave them with a positive view of the day's efforts.

YOUTH RUGBY COACHING

Professional coaches measure success in rings. College coaches measure success in championships. High School coaches measure success in titles. Youth coaches measure success in smiles.

USA Youth Coach

This section will concentrate on the one bracket of rugby coaching that I spend a significant amount of my free time working within: youth rugby. I hope it will not come across to the reader as a polemic on the state of the Youth Rugby Nation, but merely a personal view of what I see as some issues concerning coaches within the youth game today. It does not contain any coaching notes, drills or a means to secure national domination; however, it should allow those of us who work within the youth game a chance to pause and reflect about what we do with our young charges, in the hope that the structures can work more beneficially for the players.

Coaching youth rugby presents its own unique challenges and, over recent years, I have had cause to examine my own approach to the varying roles I have had within the youth game. In those navel-gazing hours there are cold-sweat moments when it has all gone dreadfully wrong, but through those times comes clarity and a resolve to improve. What follows are five discussion points that I want to just throw out there in the hope that maybe some thoughts can be taken on how we all approach the youth game.

What is the best use of guest coaches?

A few years ago I asked a very experienced coach if I could have ten minutes of his time to discuss a point of coaching that I was having some difficulty with. He graciously agreed and, as is the norm with good rugby coaches, the ten minutes turned into two hours of vigorous debate. At the end of the talk, he asked me would I be willing to hear the best advice ever on how to become an elite coach. Naively, I waited with bated breath for the secret to great coaching.

> The secret to becoming a world class coach, Eamonn, is to enrol on a course at Bath University where they teach you to speak with a Kiwi accent!

Far from deriding our southern hemisphere colleagues, he was criticizing people's belief that everything outside your club was good and what you have inside your club was bad. I regret to report that, in relative terms, the principle still remains true today within youth rugby – are high-profile coaches always better than local ones when it come to coaching youth players?

Coming into a grassroots environment as a high-profile guest coach, you will get the first ten minutes for free – you can say or do what you like and the children will think you are fine – but after that, you had better be good at your job and you had better be empathetic! Not all elite coaches can empathize with the performers several levels below and often players believe they have learned nothing, which, considering the money paid out, is a terrible shame.

Choose your guest coach carefully. There are some wonderful professional coaches in the game but all clubs need to choose a visiting coach who can add something special to their club and coaching environment – and if that person is a high-profile coach, then it can be excellent addition to your coaching year. However, there may already be a guy at a club somewhere closer and in the area who may be able to pitch that 'best practice' at your players' level much better and with greater empathy for what you are trying to coach them.

Coach development

> Take time to gather up the past so that you will be able to draw from your experiences and invest them in the future.
>
> Jim Rohn

Never before has so much information been available to help coaches prosper. Coaching courses are very much tailored to your own personal ambitions and, via the Internet, coaching newsletters, YouTube and various file-sharing resource sites, it is almost impossible not to find what you are looking for. Areas of the game at the top level change on a weekly basis and to keep up with current trends in the game, you need constantly to network and challenge your own perspective. So once a year, surround yourself with like-minded, committed individuals who enjoy travelling to events and attend some coach development workshops!

But this will only get you half-way to your ambitions. The other area of coach development is what you do with the information you have gained. Creating a style to suit yourself and your team is a key ingredient. You know your players better than anyone so how you put that information across to them is so important. You must personalize that information and teach it at a rate that can be easily digested by your team. Sometimes, a session you have watched at a coach development workshop may take you a whole season to develop, but that's acceptable as the players are learning something that will aid their progress.

Parental communication

If you are a part of a representative team or a talented working group, I have found that the best promoters or detractors of your programme are the parents and guardians of the players who work within your system. There are people who say that parents are a nightmare to deal with and your only job is to coach their children. I am not sure which structure you work in, but the days of parents not being involved fully in their children's lives have long gone – if it ever was the case in the first place.

'So what?' you may ask. 'I am not a slave to my players' parents.' That is correct – you are there to coach and your team is not a charity looking after waifs and strays. However, by communicating effectively with the parents and the people in your players' lives, you will be surprised how much goodwill is available. I cannot tell you how many times I have been contacted by parents telling me about their sons' injuries, physio appointments, club dinners, etc., which all affect the demands on my players' time – I would not normally have been informed about these if I hadn't encouraged this two-way dialogue.

In a modern empathetic arena of trust and welfare, create an environment where players want to attend. Parents will also buy into the process by being active participants and, although there are times when these conversations do become difficult, all things being equal, I would rather speak to parents than not. On match days, the pressure is sometimes lifted on a coach when all of the stakeholders become active participants in their sons' day, having been completely involved at all stages to this point. They understand the sacrifices the coaches have made in helping their children and it is very much appreciated.

One final thought

A colleague of mine was at a Senior High School dinner when a high-profile college coach uttered the following:

> To be a great coach you have to believe that you are the greatest thing in the world – with a nagging internal voice that says you actually are not.

I leave you with that to ponder.

Index of Drills by Player Position

ACTIVITY	PG No	1	2	3	4	5	6	7	8	9	10	11	12	13	14	15
THE WARM-UP																
Sprint Relays	10															
Leg and Lower Back Warm-Up for Rucking	11															
Physical Intensity	12															
Pre-Match Warm-Ups	13															
Ruck Warm-Up on Hard Ground	14															
Use the Field (1): Aerobic Runs	15	*ALL ACTIVITIES ARE SUITABLE FOR ALL PLAYING POSITIONS BUT PLAYER POSITION MAY REQUIRE ADJUSTMENT TIME UNDERTAKEN OR DISTANCE COVERED BY EACH PLAYER*														
Use the Field (2): Aerobic Interval Training	16															
Use the Field (3): Chase Sprints	17															
Use the Field (4): Staggered Sprints	18															
Use the Field (5): Dynamic Warm-Up Channels	19															
PASSING																
Basic Passing (1)	22															
Basic Passing: Balance	23															
Basic Passing (2)	24															
Basic Passing: Fatigue	25	*ALL ACTIVITIES SUITABLE FOR ALL POSITIONS*														
Basic Passing (3)	26															
High Intensity Passing: Fatigue	27															
High Pressure Passing: Space	28															
Scrum Half Passing	29									X						
Continuous Reaction Drill for 10s	30										X					
Channel Running	31															
Clearing Pass (1)	32															
Clearing Pass (2)	33															
Clearing Pass: Messy Ball	34															
Running from Depth (1)	35															
Running from Depth (2)	36															
Running from Depth (3)	37															
Three vs. Two	38	*ALL ACTIVITIES SUITABLE FOR ALL POSITIONS*														
Running from Depth (4)	39															
Starting the Scan	40															
Random Attack and Defence	41															
Attack the Space (1)	42															
Attack the Space (2)	43															
Beat the Full Back	44															
Reaction and Communication	45															
The 'No-Look' Pass	46									X	X	X	X	X	X	X
High Intensity Drill: Fatigue	47	*ALL ACTIVITIES SUITABLE FOR ALL POSITIONS*														
Loop Attack	48									X	X	X	X	X	X	X
THE BREAKDOWN																
Ball Placement Practice	51															
Basic Body Height Drill	52	*ALL ACTIVITIES SUITABLE FOR ALL POSITIONS*														
Basic Ball Placement	53															
Basic Ruck Securer Drill	54															